Vag

GW01398583

Axel Munthe

Alpha Editions

This edition published in 2024

ISBN : 9789362092830

Design and Setting By
Alpha Editions
www.alphaedis.com
Email - info@alphaedis.com

As per information held with us this book is in Public Domain.
This book is a reproduction of an important historical work. Alpha Editions uses the
best technology to reproduce historical work in the same manner it was first
published to preserve its original nature. Any marks or number seen are left
intentionally to preserve its true form.

Contents

INSTEAD OF A PREFACE

He who has written these pages is no author; his life belongs to reality, and does not leave him any peace for indulging in fiction, and, besides, he has for nearly twenty years limited his best thoughts and efforts to that special authorship which has for its only public apothecaries. He thought it very easy and refreshing to write this little book. The only difficulty about it has been to find a title, for it turned out that, when confronted with this problem, neither the writer nor any of the friends he consulted could say what stuff it was that the book was made of—was it essays, stories, or what? Essays is much too important a word for me to use, and stories it certainly is not, for I cannot remember having ever tried to invent anything.

Besides, isn't it so that in a story something always happens—and here, as a rule, very little seems to me to happen. I do not know, but can it be that it is life itself which "happens" in these pages, life as seen by an individual who can but try to be as the Immortal Gods created him, since conventionality long ago has given up in despair all hope of licking him into shape?

Now I want to tell you what made me publish this book—what made me write it cannot interest you. One day I found sitting in my consulting-room a young lady with a huge parcel on her knee. I asked her what I could do for her, and she began by telling me a long tale of woe about herself. She said that nothing interested her, nothing amused her, she was bored to death by everything and everybody. She could get anything she wished to have, she could go anywhere she liked, but she did not wish for anything, she did not want to go anywhere.

Her life was passed in idle luxury, useless to herself and to everybody else, said she. Her parents had ended by dragging her from one physician to another: one had prescribed Egypt, where they had spent the whole winter; another Cannes, where they had bought a big villa; a third India and Japan, which they had visited in their fine yacht. "But you are the only doctor who has done me any good," she said. "I have felt more happiness during this past week than I have done for years. I owe it to you, and I have come to thank you for it." She began rapidly to unfasten her parcel, and I stared at her in amazement while she produced from it one big doll after another, and quite unceremoniously placed them in a row on my writing-table amongst all my books and papers. There were twelve dolls in all, and you never saw such dolls. Some of them were dressed in well-fitting tailor-made jackets and skirts; some were evidently off for a yachting trip in blue serge suits and sailor hats; some wore smart silk dresses covered with lace and frills, and hats trimmed with huge ostrich feathers; and some looked as if they had only just returned from the Queen's Drawing-room.

I am accustomed to have queer people in my consulting-room, and I thought I noticed something glistening in her eyes. "You see, Doctor," said she with uncertain voice, "I never thought I could be of any good to anybody. I used to send money to charities at home, but all I did was to write out a cheque, and I cannot say I ever felt the slightest satisfaction in doing it. The other day I happened to come across that article about Toys in an old *Blackwood's Magazine*,[1] and since then I have been working from morning till evening to dress up all these dolls for the poor children you spoke about. I have done it all by myself, and I have felt so strangely happy the whole time."

And I, who had forgotten all about this little escapade from the toil of my everyday life, I looked at the sweet face smiling through the tears, I looked at the long row of dolls who stared approvingly at me from among all my medical paraphernalia on the writing-table. And for the first and last time in my life did I feel the ineffable joy of literary triumph, for the first and last time in my life did I feel that mystic power of being able to move others.

A smart carriage was waiting for her at the door, but we sent it away, and I put the kind donor and some of her dolls in a cab, and I remember we went to see Petruccio. I could see by her shyness that it was the first time she had entered the home of the poor. She gave each child a magnificent doll, and she blushed with delight when she saw the little sisters' beaming faces and heard the poor mother's "God bless you!" Hardly had a week passed before she brought me another dozen of dolls, and twelve more sick and destitute children forgot all about their misery. At Christmas I got up a big festa at the Jardin-des-Plantes quarter, where most of the poor Italians live, and the Christmas-tree was loaded with dolls of all sizes and descriptions. She went on bringing me more and more dolls, and there came a time when I did not know what to do with them, for I had more dolls than patients. Every chair and table in my rooms was occupied by a doll, and people asked me to show them "the dear children," and when I told them I was a bachelor and had not got any they would not believe me. To tell you the truth, when spring came I sent the lady to St. Moritz for change of air. I have never seen her since, but should she come across this book she may know that it was she and her dolls who decided its publication, and it is in her honour I have given the Toy article the first place.

There is nothing like success. Some time ago I received a letter from a man I do not know, who wrote me that he was the mayor of a large town. He said that after having read a little paper called "For those who love Music"[2] he had revoked the order which forbade organ-grinders to play in the streets of his town, and had told his children always to give the old man a penny, for "perhaps it is Don Gaetano!" I admit I was immensely flattered by this, and in honour of the kind mayor I have placed his paper second.

But is this to be the end of my literary fame, or will any other laurel-leaf mark some hitherto unpublished page of this volume? What about "Blackcock-shooting"? Will ever an English mother write to me that she is teaching her son that he can grow up every inch a man without having ever killed a half-tame pheasant or a grouse, or stealthily crept up to murder a beautiful stag?

I have not heard from the Germans in Capri yet, but when that letter comes I believe my literary ambition will have reached its zenith, and that I shall relapse into silence again.

ROME, *Spring* 1898.

TOYS

FROM THE PARIS HORIZON

In Paris the New Year is awakened by the laughter of children, the dawn of its first day glows in rosy joy on small round cheeks, and lit up by the light from children's sparkling eyes, the curtain rises upon the fairy world of toys.

This world of toys is a faithful miniature of our own, the same perpetual evolution, the same struggle for existence, goes on there as here. Types rise and vanish just as with us; the strongest and best-fitted individuals survive, defying time, whilst the weaker and less gifted are supplanted and die out.

To the former, for instance, belongs the doll, whose individual type centuries may have modified, but whose idea is eternal, whose soul lives on with the imperishable youth of the gods. The doll is thousands of years old; it has been found in the graves of little Roman children, and the archæologists of coming generations will find it amongst the remains of our culture. The children of Pompeii and Herculaneum used to trundle hoops just as you and I did when we were small, and who knows whether the rocking-horse on which we rode as boys is not a lineal descendant of that proud charger into whose wooden flanks the children of Francis I. dug their heels. The drum is also inaccessible to the variation of time; through centuries it has beaten the Christmas and New Year's day's reveille in the nursery to the battles of the tin-soldiers, and it will continue to beat as long as there are boys' arms to wield the drum-sticks and grown-up people's tympanums to be deafened. The tin-soldier views the future with calm; he will not lay down his arms until the day of the general disarmament, and we are still a long way from universal peace. Neither will the toy-sword disappear; it is the nursery-symbol of the ineradicable vice of our race, the lust for fighting. Foolscap-crowned and bell-ringing harlequins will also defy time; they will exist in the toy-world as long as there are fools in our world. Gold-laced knights with big swords at their sides, curly-locked princesses with satin shoes on dainty feet, stalwart musketeers with top boots and big moustachios—all are types which still hold their own pretty well. The Japanese doll is as yet young, but a brilliant future lies before her.

Amongst the toy-people who are gradually diminishing may be mentioned monks, hobgoblins, and kings—an evil omen for the matter of that. I don't wish to make any one uneasy, but it is a fact that the demand for kings has considerably decreased of late—my studies in toy-anthropology do not allow me the slightest doubt on this subject. It is not for me to try to explain the cause of this serious phenomenon—I understand well that this topic is a painful one, and shall not persist.

Hobgoblins—who in our world are growing more and more ill at ease since the locomotives began to pant through the forests, and who have sought and found a refuge in the toy-world, in picture-books, and fairy-tales—they begin to decrease, even they; they do not leap any longer with the same wild energy when they are let loose out of their boxes, and they do not know how to inspire the same terrifying respect as before. They are doomed to die; a few generations more and wet-nurses and nursery-maids will be studying physics, and then there will be an end to hobgoblins and Jack-in-the-boxes! For my part I shall regret them.

Our social life expresses itself even through toys, and the rising generation writes the history of its civilisation in the children's books. Our age is the age of scientific inquiry, and its sons have no time for dreams; the generation which is growing up moves in a world of thought totally different from ours. Nowadays Tom Thumb is left to take care of himself in the trackless forest, and poor Robinson Crusoe, with whom we kept such faithful company, is feeling more and more lonely on his desert island with our common friend Friday and the patient goat whose neck we so often patted in our dreams. Nowadays boy-thoughts travel with Phileas Fogg *Round the World in Eighty Days*, or undertake fearlessly a journey to the moon with carefully calculated pace of I don't know how many miles in a second, and their knapsacks stuffed with physical science. Nowadays a little future Edison sits meditating in his nursery laboratory, trying to stun a fly beneath the bell of a little air-pump, or he communicates with his little sister by means of a lilliputian telephone—when we only knew how to besiege toy-fortresses with pop-guns and arrange tin-soldiers' battles, limiting our scientific inquiries to that bloodless vivisection which consisted in ripping up the stomachs of all our dolls and pulling to pieces everything we came across to find out what was inside. These scientific toys were almost unknown some ten years ago,— these *jouets scientifiques* which now rank so high in toy-shops, and offer perhaps the greatest attraction for the children of the present. *The tranquillity of parents and the education of children* is the device on these toys—yes, there is no doubt that the children's instruction has been thought of, but their imagination, what is to become of that, now that even Christmas presents give lessons in chemistry and physics? And all this artificially increased modern thirst for knowledge, does it not destroy the germ of romance which was implanted in the child's mind? does it not drive away that rosy poetry of dreamland which is the morning glow of the awakening thought? Maybe I am wrong, but it sometimes seems to me that there is less laughter in the nurseries now than before, that the children's faces are growing more earnest. And if I am to be quite frank I must confess that I fight rather shy of these modern toys, and have never bought any of them for my little friends.

The same claim for reality which has brought forward these scientific toys is also shown in the multitude of political characters one comes across in the toy-world—Bismarck, with his bloodshot eyes and three tufts of hair; the "Zulu," the "Boer," etc. etc. The famous Tonquin treasures have not yet been brought to light, but we have long ago made acquaintance with the Tonquinese and his long nose like Mons. Jules Ferry; and the recent trouble in the Balkan states resulted in last year's novelty, *le cri de Bulgare*.[3]

Do not, however, imagine that the *rôle* of politics in the toy-world is limited to this—it is far more extensive, far more important. I now mean to dwell on this question for a moment or two, and wish to say a few words concerning *the political agitations of the toy-world*.

The political agitations of the toy-world—a weighty, and hitherto rather neglected topic—are like the swell, following the political storms which agitate our own world. The horizon which here opens before the eyes of the observer is, however, too vast to be framed in this small paper. I therefore propose to limit the subject to *the French toy-politics after l'année terrible* (1870-71).

The war between Germany and France is over long ago, but the toy-world still resounds with the echo of the clash of arms of 1870; fighting still continues with unabated ardour in the lilliputian world, where the Bismarcks and the Moltkes of the German toy-manufactories each Christmas fight new battles with *l'Article de Paris*.

Victorious by virtue of their cheapness, the Germans advance. From the Black Forest descend every Christmas hordes of wooden oxen, sheep, horses, and dogs to measure themselves against the wares of the wood-carvers of the Vosges (*St. Claude, etc. etc.*). From Hamburg, Nuremburg, and Berlin emigrate every winter thousands of dolls to dispute the favour of the buyers with their French colleagues, and every Christmas dense squadrons of spike-helmeted Prussian tin-soldiers cross the Rhine to invade the toy-shops and nurseries of France. The struggle is unequal, the competition too great. Siebenburgen and Tyrol furnish at will a complete chemist's shop, a plentifully-supplied grocery store, or a well-stocked farm with crops and implements, cows, sheep, and goats grazing on the verdant pasture, for three francs fifty centimes. Hamburg at the same moderate price offers a doll irreproachable to the superficial observer, a doll with glass eyes, curly hair, and one change of clothes, whilst the little Parisienne has already spent double that sum on her toilet alone, and therefore cannot condescend to be yours for less than half a louis d'or. Nuremburg mobilises a whole regiment of tin-soldiers, baggage waggons, and artillery (Krupp model), included, at the same price for which the toy-arsenals of Marais set on foot one single battalion of "Chasseurs d'Afrique."

The situation is gloomy—the French toys retire all along the line.

But France will never be annihilated! And if the depths of a French tin-soldier's soul were sounded, there would be found under the surface of reserve exacted by discipline, the same glorious dreams of revenge which inspired the volunteers raised by Gambetta from out of the earth. The French tin-soldier looks towards the east; he knows that he is still powerless to stop the invasion of the German toy-hordes—he is bound by Article 4 in the Frankfort treaty of peace, but he bides his time.[4]

And Revenge is near. This time also the signal for rising has been given from Belleville, by a Gambetta of the toy-world. Some years ago a poor workman at Belleville got a sudden idea, an idea that since then has engendered an army which would realise the dream of eternal peace, and keep in check the assembled troops of all Europe were it a question of number alone. He sets on foot 5,000,000 soldiers a year. The origin of these soldiers is humble, but so was Napoleon's. They spring from old sardine boxes. Thrown away on the dust-heap, the sardine box is saved from annihilation by the dust-man, who sells it to a rag-merchant in Belleville or Buttes Chaumont, who in his turn disposes of it to a specialist, who prepares it for the manufactories. The warriors are cut out of the bottom of the box. The lid and sides are used for making guns, railway-carriages, bicycles, etc. etc. All this may seem to you very unimportant at first sight, but there is now in Belleville a large manufactory founded on this idea of utilising old sardine boxes, which occupies no less than two hundred workmen and produces every year over two milliards of tin toys. I went there the other day, and no one suspecting that I was a political correspondent, I was admitted without difficulty to view the gigantic arsenal and its 5,000,000 warriors. The poor workman out of whose head the fully-armed tin-soldiers sprung—*viâ* the sardine box—is now a rich man, and, what is more, an eager and keen-sighted patriot, who in his sphere has deserved well of his country. After retreating for years the French tin-soldiers once more advance; the German spiked-helmets retire every Christmas from the conquered positions in French nurseries, and maybe the time is not far off when the tricolour shall wave over the toy-shops of Berlin—a small revanche *en attendant* the great one.

Many years have elapsed since the enemy placed his heel upon the neck of fallen France, but still to-day Paris is the metropolis of human culture. Competition has led the Article de Paris to a commercial Sedan, and from a financial point of view *le jouet Parisien* no longer belongs to the great powers of the toy-world. But the Paris doll will never admit the superiority of her German rival; she bears the stamp of nobility on her brow, and she means to rule the doll-world as before by right of her undisputed rank and her artistic refinement. It surely needs very little human knowledge to distinguish her at once, the graceful Parisienne with her *fin sourire* and her expressive eyes, from one of the dull beauties of Nuremburg or Hamburg, who, by the stereotyped grin on her carmine lips, and the staring, vacant eyes, immediately reveals her Teutonic origin. Should any hesitation be possible a glance at her feet will suffice—the Parisienne's foot is small and dainty, and she is always shod with a certain coquetry, whilst the daughter of Germany is characteristically careless of her *chaussure*—*tout comme chez nous*, for the matter of that. As for the rest of her wardrobe—to leave the anthropological side of the question—Germany, in spite of her war indemnity of five milliards, is incapable of producing a tasteful doll-toilet; the delicate fingers of a Paris grisette are required for this. It is therefore considered the proper thing among German dolls of fashion to import their dresses from some doll-Worth in Paris. I can even tell you in parenthesis that the really distinguished German dolls not only send to Paris for their dresses but also for their heads. The German doll manufacturers, incapable themselves of producing pretty and expressive doll faces, buy their dolls' heads by retail from the porcelain factories of Montreux and St. Maurice, where they are modelled by first-rate artists, such as a Carrier-Belleuse and others.

Up till now I have confined myself to the upper classes of doll society, but even amongst the well-to-do middle-class dolls of ten to fifteen francs apiece, the difference between German and French is palpable at first sight. The further one descends into the lower regions of society, in the doll *bourgeoisie*, the less clear becomes the national type. I will undertake, however, to recognise my French friend even amongst dolls of five francs apiece. To determine the nationality of a one-franc doll, it is necessary to possess great preliminary knowledge and much natural aptitude. For the benefit of future explorers in these still obscure regions of anthropology I may here point out an important item in the necessary physical examination—the doll must be shaken. If there is a rattling inside she is probably French, for the Paris grisettes who make these dolls have a habit of putting some pebbles inside them, which, I am told, tends to develop the taste for vivisection amongst the rising generation.

Lower down in the series where the transition type of Darwin is found, where the doll is without either arms or legs, and where every trace of soul has died out from her impassive wooden face, stamped with the same passion-free calm which characterises the marble folk of antiquity, or where an unconscious smile alone glides over the rudimentary features into which the wax has hardened, where the nose is nothing but a prophetic outline, and where the black eyes are still shaded by the chaotic darkness out of which the first doll rose—there all national distinctions cease, there the embryo doll lives her life of Arcadian simplicity, undisturbed by all political agitations in the land which gave her birth; the doll *à treize sous* does not emigrate, maybe from patriotic motives, maybe from lack of initiative.[5] Her rôle in life is humble; she belongs to the despised. Her place in the large toy-shops is in a dark corner behind the other dolls, who stretch forth their jointed arms towards better-to-do purchasers, and with gleaming glass eyes and laughing lips appropriate the admiring glances of all the customers. But far away in the deserted streets of the suburbs, where the whole toy-shop consists of a portable table and the public of a crowd of ragged urchins,—there the doll *à treize sous* reigns supreme. By the flickering light of the lantern illuminating the modest fairy-world which Christmas and the New Year display to the children of the poor, there the despised doll becomes beautiful as a queen and is surrounded by her whole court of admirers.

And I myself am one of her admirers. Not one of the fashionable beauties of the Magasin du Louvre has ever made my heart beat one whit the faster; not one of the charming coquettes of the Bon Marché has succeeded in catching me in the net of her blond tresses; but I admit the tender sympathy with which my eyes rest upon the coarse features of the doll *à treize sous*. Every one to his taste—I think she is handsome; I cannot help it. And we have often met; chance leads me frequently across her path. But fancy if it were not chance! fancy if instead it was my undeclared affection which so often guided my steps to these places where I knew I should meet my sweetheart! fancy if I were falling in love at last! At all events I haven't said anything to her, nor has she ever said a word to me either of encouragement or rebuff. But, as I said before, we often meet at the houses of mutual friends, and sometimes, especially at Christmas and New Year, have we come together there. My visit does not impress them very much, but what happiness does not the doll spread around her! Realising my subordinate rôle I willingly bow before the superior social talents of my companion, and silently in a corner by myself I enjoy her success. I don't know how she manages it, but she has hardly crossed the threshold before it seems to grow brighter inside the dark garret where live the children of destitution. The light radiates from the sparkling eyes of the little ones, glimmers in a faint smile on the pale cheek of the sick brother, and falls like a halo round the bald head of the doll. The little fellow crawling on the floor suddenly ceases his sobbing; he forgets that he is hungry, forgets that he is cold, and with radiant joy he stretches out his arms to welcome the unexpected guest. And later at night, when it is time for me to go away, when the children of the rich have danced themselves tired round the Christmas tree, when the soldier's bugle has sounded in the boys' nursery, and when the little girls' smart dolls have been put to sleep each in their dainty bed—then little sister up in the garret tenderly wraps mother's ragged shawl round her beloved doll, for the night is cold and the doll has nothing on; and so they fall asleep side by side together, the pauper doll and her grateful little admirer.

Despised and ridiculed by us grown-up people, whose eyes have been led astray by the modern demand for realism, it is nevertheless a fact that the doll *à treize sous* in the freshness of her primitive naïveté approaches nearer the ideal than the costly beauties of the Louvre and Bon Marché, who have reached the highest summit of refinement. We grown-up people have lost the faculty of understanding this from the moment we lost the simplicity of our childhood, but our teacher in this, as in many other things, is the little chap who still crawls about on the floor. Put a smart doll of fashion side by side with a simple pauper doll whose shape is as yet barely human, and you will see that the child usually stretches out his arms towards the latter. It sounds like a paradox, but it is a fact that you can easily verify for yourself; these cheap toys are, as a rule, preferred even by the children of the rich— that is to say, so long as they are real children and unconscious of the value of money. Later on, when they have acquired this knowledge, they are driven out from the Eden of childhood, their eyes are opened to the nakedness of the pauper doll, and what I have just said ceases to be true.

But the "political agitations"—what has become of them? Far away from all political storms and quarrels, my thoughts have fled to the garret idyll of the pauper doll; I have tried to sketch her as she has so often revealed herself to me; I have lifted a corner of the veil of unmerited oblivion which conceals her humble existence, there where she lives to bring joy to those whom the world rears to sorrow. I have done so as a tribute of gratitude for the pure joy which she has so often given me also, although I am myself too old to play with dolls. But, thank God, I am not too old to look on!

The doll is not old, and old age will never touch her—she will never grow old; she dies young, even as the hero, beloved of the gods. She dies young, and the first few weeks of the New Year have hardly passed away before she wends her way to the strange Elysian fields, where all that survives of broken toys sleeps under the shade of withered Christmas trees.

FOR THOSE WHO LOVE MUSIC

I had engaged him by the year. Twice a week he came and went through his whole répertoire, and lately, out of sympathy for me, he would play the Miserere of the *Trovatore*, which was his show piece, twice over. He stood there in the middle of the street looking steadfastly up at my windows while he played, and when he had finished he would take off his hat with a "Addio Signor!"

It is well known that the barrel-organ, like the violin, gets a fuller and more sympathetic tone the older it is. The old artist had an excellent instrument, not of the modern noisy type which imitates a whole orchestra with flutes and bells and beats of drums, but a melancholy old-fashioned barrel-organ which knew how to lend a dreamy mystery to the gayest allegretto, and in whose proudest tempo di Marcia there sounded an unmistakable undertone of resignation. And in the tenderer pieces of the répertoire, where the melody, muffled and staggering like a cracked old human voice, groped its way amongst the rusty pipes of the treble, then there was a trembling in the bass like suppressed sobs. Now and then the voice of the tired organ failed it completely, and then the old man would resignedly turn the handle during some bars of rest more touching in their eloquent silence than any music.

True, the instrument was itself very expressive, but the old man had surely his share in the sensation of melancholy which came over me whenever I heard his music. He had his beat in the poor quarter behind the Jardin des Plantes, and many times during my solitary rambles up there had I stopped and taken my place among the scanty audience of ragged street boys which surrounded him.

We made acquaintance one misty dark autumn day. I sat on a bench under the fading trees, which in vain had tried to deck the gloomy square with a little summer, and now hopelessly suffered their leaves to fall; and, like a melancholy accompaniment to my dreamy thoughts, the old barrel-organ in the slum close by coughed out the aria from the last act of the Traviata: "Addio del passato bei sogni ridenti!"

I startled as the music stopped. The old man had gone through his whole répertoire, and after a despairing inspection of his audience he resignedly tucked the monkey under his cloak and prepared to depart. I have always liked barrel-organs, and I have a sufficiently correct ear to distinguish good music from bad; so I went up and thanked him and asked him to play a little longer, unless he was too tired in the arm. I am afraid he was not spoiled by praise, for he looked at me with a sad, incredulous expression which pained me, and with an almost shy hesitation he asked me if it was any special piece I wished to hear. I left the choice to the old man. After a mysterious manipulation with some screws under the organ, which was answered from its depths by a half-smothered groan, he began slowly and with a certain solemnity to turn the handle, and with a friendly glance at me, he said, "*Questo è per gli amici.*"[6]

It was a tune I had not heard him play before, but I knew well the sweet old melody, and half aloud I searched my memory for the words of perhaps the finest folk-song of Naples:

"Fenestra che luciva e mò non luce Segn' è ca Nenna mia stace malata S' affaccia la sorella e me lo dice: Nennella toja è morta e s' è aterrata Chiagneva sempe ca dormeva sola, Mò dorme in distìnta compagnia."

He looked at me with a shy interest while he played, and when he had finished he bared his gray head; I also raised my hat, and thus our acquaintance was made.

It was not difficult to see that times were hard—the old man's clothes were doubtful, and the pallor of poverty lay over his withered features, where I read the story of a long life of failure. He came from the mountains around Monte Cassino, so he informed me, but where the monkey hailed from I never quite got to know.

Thus we met from time to time during my rambles in the poor quarters. Had I a moment to spare I stopped for a while to listen to a tune or two, as I saw that it gratified the old man, and since I always carried a lump of sugar in my pocket for any dog acquaintance I might possibly meet, I soon made friends with the monkey also. The relations between the little monkey and her impresario were unusually cordial, and this notwithstanding that she had completely failed to fulfil the expectations which had been founded upon her—she had never been able to learn a single trick, the old man told me. Thus all attempts at education had long ago been abandoned, and she sat there huddled together on her barrel-organ and did nothing at all. Her face was sad, like that of most animals, and her thoughts were far away. But now and then she woke up from her dreams, and her eyes could then take a suspicious, almost malignant expression, as they lit upon some of the street boys who crowded round her tribune and tried to pull her tail, which stuck out from her little gold-laced garibaldi. To me she was always very amiable; confidently she laid her wrinkled hand in mine and absently she accepted the little attentions I was able to offer her. She was very fond of sweetmeats, and burnt almonds were, in her opinion, the most delectable thing in the world.

Since the old man had once recognised his musical friend on a balcony of the Hôtel de l'Avenir, he often came and played under my windows. Later on he became engaged, as already said, to come regularly and play twice a week,—it may, perhaps, appear superfluous for one who was studying medicine, but the old man's terms were so small, and you know I have always been so fond of music. Besides it was the only recreation at hand—I was working hard in the Hôtel de l'Avenir, for I was to take my degree in the spring.

So passed the autumn, and the hard time came. The rich tried on the new winter fashions, and the poor shivered with the cold. It became more and more difficult for well-gloved hands to leave the warm muff or the fur-lined coat to take out a copper for the beggar, and more and more desperate became the struggle for bread amongst the problematical existences of the street. Before hopelessly-closed windows small half-frozen artistes gave concerts in the courtyards; unnoticed resounded the most telling pieces of the répertoire about *La bella Napoli* and *Santa Lucia*, while stiffened fingers twanged the mandoline, and the little sister, shivering with cold, banged the tambourine. In vain the old street-singer sang with hoarse pathos the song about *La Gloire* and *La Patrie*, and in vain my friend played that piece *per gli amici*—thicker and thicker fell the snowflakes over the humbly-bared heads, and scarcer and scarcer fell the coppers into the outstretched hats.

Now and then I came across my friend, and we always had, as before, a kind word for one another. He was now wrapped up in an old Abruzzi cloak, and I noticed that the greater the cold became the faster did he turn the handle to keep himself warm; and towards December the Miserere itself was performed in allegretto.

The monkey had now become civilian, and wrapped up her little thin body in a long ulster such as Englishmen wear; but she was fearfully cold notwithstanding, and, forgetful of all etiquette, more and more often she jumped from the barrel-organ and crept in under the old man's cloak.

And while they were suffering out there in the cold I sat at home in my cosy, warm room, and instead of helping them, I forgot all about them, more and more taken up as I was with my coming examination, with no thought but for myself. And then one day I suddenly left my lodgings and removed to the Hôtel Dieu to take the place of a comrade, and weeks passed before I put my foot out of the hospital.

I remember it so well, it was the very New Year's Day we met each other again. I was crossing the Place de Notre Dame, mass was just over, and the people were streaming out of the old cathedral. As usual, a row of beggars was standing before the door, imploring the charity of the churchgoers. The severe winter had increased their number, and besides the usual beggars, cripples and blind, who were always by the church porch, reciting in loud voices the history of their misery, there stood a silent rank of Poverty's accidental recruits—poor fellows whose daily bread had been buried under the snow, and whose pride the cold had at last benumbed. At the farther end, and at some distance from the others, an old man stood with bent head and outstretched hat, and with painful surprise I recognised my friend in his threadbare old coat without the Abruzzi cloak, without the barrel-organ, without the monkey. My first impulse was to go up to him, but an uneasy feeling of I do not know what held me back; I felt that I blushed and I did not move from my place. Every now and then a passer-by stopped for a moment and made as if to search his pocket, but I did not see a single copper fall into the old man's hat. The place became gradually deserted, and one beggar after another trotted off with his little earnings. At last a child came out of the church, led by a gentleman in mourning; the child pointed towards the old man, and then ran up to him and laid a silver coin in his hat. The old man humbly bowed his head in thanks, and even I, with my unfortunate absent-mindedness, was very nearly thanking the little donor also, so pleased was I. My friend carefully wrapped up the precious gift in an old pocket-handkerchief, and stooping forward, as if still carrying the barrel-organ on his back, he walked off.

I happened to be quite free that morning, and, thinking that a little walk before luncheon could do me no harm after the hospital air, I followed him at a short distance across the Seine. Once or twice I nearly caught him up, and all but tapped him on the shoulder, with a "Buon giorno, Don Gaetano!" Yet, without exactly knowing why, I drew back at the last moment and let him get a few paces ahead of me again.

An icy wind blew straight against us, and I drew my fur cloak closer round me. But just then it suddenly struck me to ask myself why, after all, it was I who owned such a warm and comfortable fur cloak, whilst the old man who tramped along in front of me had only a threadbare old coat? And why was it for me that luncheon was waiting, and not for him? Why should I have a good blazing fire burning in my cosy room, while the old man had to wander about the streets the whole day long to find his food, and in the evening go home to his miserable garret and, unprotected against the cold of the winter night, prepare for the next day's struggle for bread?

And it suddenly dawned upon me why I had blushed when I saw him at Notre Dame, and why I could not make up my mind to go and speak to him—I felt ashamed before this old man, I felt ashamed at life's unmerited generosity to me and its severity to him. I felt as if I had taken something from him which I ought to restore to him; and I began to wonder whether it might be the fur coat. But I got no further in my meditations, for the old man stopped and looked in at a shop window. We had just crossed the Place Maubert and turned into the Boulevard St. Germain; the boulevard was full of people, so that, without being noticed, I could approach him quite close.

He was standing before an elegant confectioner's shop, and to my surprise he entered without hesitation. I took up my position before the shop window, alongside some shivering street arabs who stood there, absorbed in the contemplation of the unattainable delicacies within, and I watched the old man carefully untie his pocket-handkerchief and lay the little girl's gift upon the counter. I had hardly time to draw back before he came out with a red paper bag of sweets in his hand, and with rapid steps he started off in the direction of the Jardin des Plantes.

I was very much astonished at what I had seen, and my curiosity made me follow him. He slackened his pace at one of the little slums behind Hôpital de la Pitié, and I saw him disappear into a dirty old house. I waited outside a minute or two, and then I groped my way through the pitch-dark entrance, climbed up a filthy staircase, and found a door slightly ajar. An icy, dark room, in the middle three ragged little children crouched together around a half-extinct brazier, in the corner the only furniture in the room—a clean iron bedstead, with crucifix and rosary hung on the wall above it, and by the window an image of the Madonna adorned with gaudy paper flowers; I was in Italy, in my poor, exiled Italy. And in the purest Tuscan the eldest sister informed me that Don Gaetano lived in the garret. I went up there and knocked, but no one answered, so I opened the door myself. The room was brightly lit up by a blazing fire. With his back towards the door, Don Gaetano was on his knees before the stove busy heating a little saucepan over the fire, beside him on the floor lay an old mattress with the well-known Abruzzi cloak thrown over it, and close by, spread out on a newspaper, were various delicacies—an orange, walnuts, and raisins, and there also was the red paper bag. Don Gaetano dropped a lump of sugar into the saucepan, stirred it with a stick, and in a persuasive voice I heard him say, "*Che bella roba, che bella roba, quanto è buono questa latte con lo zucchero! Non piange anima mia, adesso siamo pronti!*"[7]

A slight rustling was heard beneath the Abruzzi cloak, and a black little hand was stretched out towards the red paper bag.

"*Primo il latte, primo il latte,*" admonished the old man. "*Non importa, piglia tu una,*"[8] he repented, and took a big burnt almond out of the paper bag; the little hand disappeared, and a crunching was heard under the cloak. Don Gaetano poured the warm milk in a saucer, and then he carefully lifted up a corner of the cloak. There lay the poor little monkey with heaving breast and eyes glowing with fever. Her face had become so small, and her complexion was ashy gray. The old man took her on his knees, and tenderly as a mother he poured some spoonfuls of the warm milk into her mouth. She looked with indifferent eyes towards the delicacies on the table, and absently she let her fingers pass through her master's beard. She was so tired that she could hardly hold her head up, and now and then she coughed so that her thin little body trembled, and she pressed both her hands to her temples. Don Gaetano shook his head sadly, and carefully laid the little invalid back under the cloak.

A feeble blush spread over the old man's face as he caught sight of me. I told him that I had happened to be passing by just as he was entering his house, and that I took the liberty of following him upstairs in order to bid him good-morning and to give him my new address, in the hope that he would come and play to me as before. I involuntarily looked round for the barrel-organ as I spoke, and Don Gaetano, who understood, informed me that he no longer played the organ—he sang. I glanced at the precious pile of wood beside the fireplace, at the new blanket that hung before the window to keep out the draught, at the delicacies on the newspaper—and I also understood.

The monkey had been ill three weeks—*la febbre*, explained the old man. We knelt one at each side of the bed, and the sick animal looked at me with her mute prayer for help. Her nose was hot, as it is with sick children and dogs, her face wrinkled like that of an old, old woman, and her eyes had got quite a human expression. Her breathing was so short, and we could hear how it rattled in her throat. The diagnosis was not difficult—she had consumption. Now and again she stretched out her thin arms as if she implored us to help her, and Don Gaetano thought that she did so because she wished to be bled.[9] I would willingly have given in in this case, although opposed in principle to this treatment, if I had thought it possible that any benefit could have been derived from it; but I knew only too well how unlikely this was, and I tried my best to make Don Gaetano understand it. Unhappily I did not know myself what there was to be done. I had at that time a friend amongst the keepers of the monkey-house in the Jardin des Plantes, and the same night he came with me to have a look at her; he said that there was nothing to be done, and that there was no hope. And he was right. For one week more the fire blazed in Don Gaetano's garret, then it was left to go out, and it became cold and dark as before in the old man's home.

True, he got his barrel-organ out from the pawn-shop, and now and then a copper did fall into his hat also. He did not die of starvation, and that was about all he asked of life.

So the spring came and I left Paris; and God knows what has become of Don Gaetano.

If you happen to hear a melancholy old barrel-organ in the courtyard, go to the window and give a penny to the poor errant musician—perhaps it is Don Gaetano! If you find that his organ disturbs you, try if you like it better by making him stand a little farther off, but don't send him away with harshness! He has to hear so many hard words as it is; why should not we then be a little kind to him—we who love music?

POLITICAL AGITATIONS IN CAPRI

Don't be alarmed—they are not going to disturb the peace of Europe.

Alas! there are spots even on the sun, and neither is "the loveliest pearl in Naples' crown" altogether faultless.

Croaking ravens swarm around the ruins where thousand-year-old memories lie slumbering, dirty dwarf hands fumble amidst the remains of fallen giants' vanished splendour, barbarians pull to pieces the mosaic floors on which the feet of emperors trod. Night-capped and blue-stockinged Prose startles the Idyll which lies there dreaming with half-closed eyes, grinning fauns push aside the vines which hide from view the cool grotto where the nymph of the legend bathes her graceful limbs.

Capri is sick, Capri is infested with parasites even as the old lion. Capri is full of—yes, but in politics one has to be careful; I say nothing, read the article to the end, and you will see what it is that Capri is full of.

Amidst the ruins of Tiberius's Villa you sit on high, gazing out over the sea. Absently your eye follows a white sail in the distance; it is a little peaceful fishing-boat quietly sailing home. And your thoughts wander far, far away. Here, in his marble-shining palace, stood once upon a time the ruler of the world; he gazed out over the sea, he also, but his eye was not as fearless as yours, for he dreaded the avenger of his victims in every approaching boat; and when the bay was dark he would still linger up there and, trembling, seek to read his doom in the stars which studded the vault of heaven. No crimes could help him any longer to forgetfulness of himself; no vice could any more benumb the torture of his soul; within his rock-built citadel the sombre emperor suffered torments far greater than any he had ever inflicted on his victims; his heart had long since bled to death under his purple toga, but his soul lived on in its titanic sorrow. The spot whereon you lie is named *Il Salto di Tiberio*. From here he hurled his victims into the sea, and there below men were rowing about in boats in order to crush to death with their oars those who were still struggling with the waves. Bend over the precipice and see the foaming surge—old fishermen have told me that sometimes when the moon goes under a cloud and all is dark, the waves breaking over the rocks beneath seem tinged with blood.

But the sun streams his forgiveness over the crumbled witness of so much sin, and, ere long, the vision of the sombre emperor fades from your thought. Now it is silent and peaceful up at Villa Tiberio. You lie there on your back gazing out over the gulf, and it seems to you as though the world ended beyond its lovely shores. The restless strife of the day does not reach you here, and all dissonance is silenced; your thoughts fly aimlessly round, play for awhile amongst the surf near Sorrento's rocks, send their open-armed greeting to Ischia's groves, and pluck some fragrant roses from the verdant shore of Posilipo. So perception gradually dies away, no longer do you hear the buzz of the whirling wheels in the factory of thought—to-day is a day of rest and your soul may dream. What dream you?—You know not! Where are you?—You know not! You fly on the white wings of the sea-gulls far, far away over the wide waters; you sail with the brilliant clouds high overhead where no thought can reach you.

But you are only a prisoner after all—a prisoner who dreamt he was free and is awakened in the midst of his dreams by the rattle of a jailer's key. The sound of voices strikes your ear, and like a wing-shot bird you fall to the earth. Beside you stands a lanky individual, and he says to his companion that it is incredible that a man can be prosaic enough to fall asleep on a spot so *wunderbar*. Ah, you are asleep, are you?

The spell is broken, the harmony destroyed, and you get up to go away. He then assaults you with the question whether you don't think the gulf is blue? and you have not walked on ten yards before he attacks you treacherously from behind with the remark that the sky is also blue. You believe it helps to stare savagely at him—I have done it many times, and it does not impress him in the very least. You want to try to make him believe you are deaf— that is no use either; he takes it as a compliment, for he prefers to have the conversation all to himself.

The sun stands high in the heavens and the summer's day is so warm—come, let us go and bathe in the cool water of the blue grotto. No, my friend, not there! Even thither, like sharks they come swimming after us to ask us if we are aware that the blue grotto of Capri is virtually German, that it was *ein Deutscher* who discovered the grotto in 1826. Let us be off for Bagni di Tiberio, the ruins of the emperor's bath, strip off our clothes inside one of the cool little chambers which still remain amongst huge blocks of crumbling masonry, and plunge into the sapphire water. But do you see those huge holes in the fine sand,—are there elephants in the island? No, my friend, but let us be off! I know the track, and there she sits, the blonde Gretchen, reading one of Spielhagen's novels—were it Heine she was reading I might perhaps forgive her.

We return along the beach to the Marina and wend our way along the old path between the vineyards leading up to the village. Unfortunately the new carriage road is nearly ready, but we, of course, prefer the old way, by far the more picturesque of the two. On the beach we stumble over easels and colour-boxes at short distances set out as traps for dreamers; beside each trap sits an amateur in ambush under a big umbrella, and he invokes *der Teufel* to help him, which I suppose he does.

You propose putting up at Albergo Pagano—yes, you are right; it is no doubt the best hotel in the island. Old Pagano, who was a capital fellow, died many years ago, and only we old Capriotes can remember him. His son Manfredo, who now manages the hotel, is my very good friend; but it is not his fault that his house has become as German as though it lay in the heart of *Das grosse Vaterland.* At least a good fifty of them are gathered round the table in the big dining-room. Upon the walls hangs a plaster medallion of the *Kaiser* decorated with fresh laurels, and should they pay you the compliment of mistaking you for a Frenchman, it is just possible they may drink a bumper to the memory of 1870—an experience I once went through myself. Instead of the silence and the peace you so longed for, you are subjected during the whole of dinner-time to the most terrific uproar worthy of a *Kneipe* in Bremen. In despair you fling open the door leading into the garden—no, you are in Italy after all! Out there under the pergola the moonbeams are playing amongst the vines, the air is soft and caressing, and the summer evening recites to you its enchanting sonnet as a compensation for the prose within. You wander there up and down all alone, but scarcely have you had time to say to yourself that you are happy before

"Heil dir im Sieges Kranz!"

rings like a war-cry through the peaceful night, answered from the street by some little Capriote ragamuffins with a horrible chorus of

"Ach! du lieber Augustin! Augustin, Augustin!"

Of course I am aware of the supercilious way in which many of the readers of *Letters from a Mourning City*[10] have turned up their noses at my circle of friends out here—lazzaroni, shabby old monks, half-starving sailors, etc. The hour is at hand for introducing you to some acquaintances of mine of somewhat higher rank, and now I will tell you a story of the upper regions of society. It happened at Capri a good many years ago, and the *dramatis personæ* consisted of my friend D——, myself, and the then Crown Princess of Germany.

My friend D—— and I happened to be the only profane people in the hotel just then. The whole of the big dining-table was in the hands of the Germans, whilst we two sat by ourselves at a small side-table. It was there we had our little observatory, as Professor Palmieri had his on Mount Vesuvius. For some days past our keen instruments of perception had warned us that something unusual was going on at the big table. The roaring of an evening was louder than ever, the smoke rose in thicker clouds, the beer ran in streams, and the faces were flushed to red-heat—everything announced an eruption of patriotism. One evening there arrived a telegram which, amidst a terrific babel of voices, was read aloud by one of the party—a commercial traveller from Potsdam, whom I personally hated because he snored at night; his room was next to mine and the walls of the hotel were thin. The telegram announced that the Crown Princess of Germany, who had been spending the last few days in Naples, was expected to visit Capri the next day in the strictest incognito. Nobody appeared to understand that the word "incognito" means that one wishes to be left in peace, and during the rest of the dinner the faithful patriots did nothing but discuss the best way of how to spoil the unfortunate Princess's little visit to the island. A complete programme was drawn up there and then: a triumphal arch was to be erected, a select deputation was to swoop down upon her the moment she set foot on land, while the main body was to block her way up to the piazza. Patriotic songs were to be sung in chorus, a speech read, whilst the commercial traveller from Potsdam was to express in a welcoming poem what already his face said eloquently enough—that poetry was not in his line. Every garden in Capri was to be despoiled of its roses, whole bushes and trees were to be uprooted wherewith to deck the triumphal arch, and all night they were to weave garlands and stitch flags.

I went up to my room, threw myself on the sofa, and lit a cigarette. And as I lay there meditating, feelings of the deepest compassion towards the Crown Princess of Germany began to overwhelm me. I had just read in the papers how, during her stay in Naples, she had sought by every manner of means to elude all official recognition, and to avoid every sort of demonstration in her honour during her excursions round the bay. Poor Princess! she had flattered herself upon having left all weary court etiquette behind in foggy Berlin, and yet she was not to be allowed to enjoy in peace one single summer day on the gulf! To be rich enough to be able to buy the whole of Capri, and yet be unable to enjoy the peaceful idyll of the enchanting island for one short hour! To be destined to wear one of the proudest crowns of the world, and yet to be powerless to prevent a commercial traveller from writing poetry! My compassionate reflections were here disturbed by the noise of heavy footsteps in the adjoining room; it sounded like the tramp of horses' hoofs; it was the "*Probenreiter*" who mounted his Pegasus. The whole night through I lay there reflecting on the vanity of earthly power, and the whole night did the Poet Laureate wander up and down his room. Once the tramping ceased, and there was a silence. There was a panting from within, and I heard a husky voice murmur—

"Ich stehe hier auf Felsenstrand! Ich stehe hier auf Felsenstrand!"[11]

A moment afterwards I heard him fling open his window and let the night air cool the fire of his inspiration. Our rooms opened on to the same balcony, and carefully lifting up my blind I could see the moonlight falling full upon him as he leaned against the window-frame. His hair stood on end and an inarticulate mumble fell from his lips. He gazed in despair up to the heavens where the stars were twinkling knowingly at one another; he glanced out over the garden where the night wind flew tittering amongst the leaves. But he never saw the joke until a startled young cock inquired of some old cocks down in the poultry yard what time it was, and then crowed straight into his face that the night was passed and he had got no further than the first verse. Then he murmured once more a plaintive—

"Ich stehe hier auf Felsenstrand!"

and banged his windows to. All the cocks of Pagano's crowed "Bravo! Bravo!" but Phoebus, Phoebus Apollo, the God of the Sun and of the poets, entered his room at that moment, and he reddened with anger when he caught sight of the commercial traveller tampering with his lyre.

Later on, when the chambermaid appeared, I heard him call out for coffee and cognac—having spent the whole night like that on his *Felsenstrand*, no wonder he needed a pick-me-up. He was late for luncheon. I glanced at the poet; an interesting pallor lent a faint look of distinction to the commercial traveller's plump features, and his great goggle eyes lay like extinct suns under his heavy eyelids. He received great attention from everybody, especially from the fair sex. I heard him confide to his neighbour at table that he always succeeded best with improvisations, and that he did not intend to let the reins of his inspiration loose until the last moment. They drank to his charming talent, whereupon he modestly smiled. He ate nothing, but drank considerably. At dessert he had regained his high colour, harangued every one excitedly, and drank toasts right and left. But it seemed as if he dared not be alone with his thoughts; as soon as the conversation around him ceased, he sank into profound meditation, and an attentive observer could easily detect that the roses of his cheeks were hiding cruel thorns which pierced his soul. For it was twelve o'clock; the Princess was expected at four, and he still stood there like Napoleon on St. Helena, alone and abandoned on his *Felsenstrand*, vainly gazing out over the unfathomable ocean of poetry in search of one single little friendly rhyme to row him over to the next verse.

The hotel had become quite unbearable downstairs; rehearsals of patriotic songs were going on in the salon, whilst in the hall went on a busy manufacture of garlands, to which the victim's name and long fluttering ribbons were being attached. The piazza was gaily decorated; the triumphal arch was ready—a black cardboard eagle perched on the top holding a white placard in his beak, upon which stood out in huge red letters the word *Willkommen*. Flag-staffs and garlands all over the piazza; even Nicolino, barber and *salassatore* (bleeder), had decided to join the triple alliance, and a colossal German flag was waving before his *salone*. I did not know what to do with myself, and at last I strolled up towards Villa di Tiberio—up there, there might be a chance of a little peace at all events. I had scarcely had time to lie down in my favourite place far out on the edge of the cliff, viewing the Bay of Naples on one side and the Bay of Salerno and the wide sea on the other, before a long shadow fell across me. I looked up, and saw a patriot staring fixedly through a telescope towards Naples. As a matter of fact, something was visible in the midst of the bay, but the haze made it difficult to see what it was. Suddenly he gave a sort of war-whoop, whereupon two other spies, who must have been sitting at the top of the old watch-tower, came bursting on the scene. I knew quite well what it was that had appeared in sight—it was the big "Scoppa-boat" sailing home from Naples.[12] Of course I said nothing, as there was always a faint hope that they might mistake it for the expected steamer, and take themselves off. But unfortunately they also guessed rightly, and all three sat down on the grass beside me, and began munching sandwiches and abusing Tiberius. I took myself off, and returned to Capri. On the piazza I came across my friend D——, who did not seem to be in a very good temper either; he was on his way to the Marina, and I accompanied him thither. Down at the Marina everything was peaceful and quiet, for the time being at all events. Old men sat there in the open boathouses mending their nets, and small boys, who had not seen fit to put on more clothes than usual for the Princess's expected visit, played about in the surf, and rolled their little bronze bodies in the sand. The landing-place was crowded as usual when the Naples steamer is expected; girls stood there offering corals, flowers, and fruit for sale, and in the rear stood patient little donkeys, ready saddled for carrying the expected visitors on a trip up to the village. We were just about to blot the whole of Germany from our minds, when my friend Alessio, shading his eyes with his hand, suddenly observed that the steamer which had just come in sight was not the usual passenger steamer from Naples, but a larger and more rapid boat. I looked at my watch, it was barely three o'clock; I had hoped for at least another hour's respite. Alessio was right; it was not the usual boat that hove in sight. And now the Marina began to wake up, and people came pouring in from all sides. We saw the deputation rush down the hill at full speed, with the chorus at its heels, and last of all came the court poet, who surely disapproved as much as we did at the Princess's anticipating her visit by a whole hour. The steamer was certainly going with a greater speed than the usual boat, and she also seemed to draw more water, as she backed farther out than usual from the harbour. The solemn moment was at hand; the deputation stood on the landing-stage in battle array, headed by the commercial traveller. We saw several people descend the ladder and step into a little boat, which rapidly made for the shore.

"Heil dir im Sieges Kranz!"

was now performed, and hardly had they got through the first verse when the boat pulled up alongside the little quay, and two ladies and a gentleman in uniform prepared to land. If they thought this would prove so easy a matter, they were mistaken—they were stopped short by the commercial traveller from Potsdam, who solemnly and warningly stretched out his right hand towards them, while with his left he drew a paper out of his trousers pocket. My old compassion for the Crown Princess rose anew, but what could I do for her? All hope of escape was at an end. . . .

"Ich stehe hier auf Felsenstrand"—

—but here there was a sudden silence. One of the ladies laughingly bent forward to say a few words to the gentleman in uniform, who quietly informed the deputation that these two ladies of the Princess's suite were anxious to make an excursion up to the village, while the Princess herself, who had remained on board, would sail round the island. At that very moment we saw the steamer turn round and make for the western side of the island.

Utterly dumbfounded, the deputation held a council of war as to the best course to be pursued. It was evident that the steamer had gone to make "*il giro*" (*i.e.* the usual round of the island), to return finally to the Grande Marina, the only real landing-place which Capri possesses. True that a sort of harbour exists also on the south side at the Piccola Marina, but it has fallen into disuse, and the road hence into the village is very rough. They therefore decided to await the steamer's return where they were; more than an hour it would scarcely take. The deputation sank dejectedly down upon some upturned boats, but the poet remained standing for fear of creasing his dress-coat (fancy wearing a dress-coat and top-hat in Capri!) And he ran no chance of freezing, I can tell you, as he stood there in his sun-bath. The hour dragged wearily along, but still no sign of the steamer. They had waited for nearly two hours, when a fisherman phlegmatically observed that as far as he could make out the steamer had gone to the Piccola Marina, for he had rowed past just as the jolly-boat set out from the steamer, and some one on the captain's bridge had asked him how many feet of water they might count upon at the Piccola Marina. Up flew the deputation as if stung by an asp, and disappeared in a cloud of dust on to the Capri road.

We dawdled about the Marina for some time longer, but finally we also wandered up to Capri, not by the broad carriage-road, but climbing the old path which joins the Anacapri road at some distance from the village, thus avoiding the piazza altogether.

It was as warm as a summer's day, and we lay down by the roadside to rest in the high grass. We talked politics by way of exception. My friend D——— is an Alsatian; he had been through the Franco-German war, and was anything but tender towards the Germans, and neither was I, for reasons of my own. But we were generous enemies, and we agreed that we were very sorry for the Crown Princess, however German she might be.

And thus I came to speak of my nocturnal adventure with the commercial traveller, and no one being within earshot it is just possible that we cracked a joke or two at the poet's expense. I remember that we tried to steer him safely through his poem, and lay there roaring with laughter, composing some extra verses to his unfinished inspiration. My old dog lay beside me in the grass; he did his best to follow us in our poetical flights, but the heat had made him somewhat indifferent to literary pursuits, and he never succeeded in keeping more than one eye open at a time. From out the ivy covering the old stone wall behind us a little quick-tailed lizard peeped every now and then to warm itself in the sun. Whenever you catch sight of one of these little lizards you should whistle softly; the graceful little animal will then stand still, gazing wonderingly around with her bright eyes to see from whence the sound proceeds. She is so frightened that you can see her heart beat in her brilliant green breast, but she is so curious and so fond of music—and there is so little music to be heard inside the old stone wall! You have only to keep quite quiet to see her emerge from her hiding-place and settle down to listen attentively. Something rather melancholy is what pleases her best; she likes Verdi, and I often start with Traviata when I give concerts for lizards. I am so fond of music myself, and maybe that is the reason why I try to be kind to these small music-lovers. That any one can have the heart to take the pretty, graceful little lizards captive is more than I can understand; they belong to an old Italian wall as much as the ivy and the sunshine. But in Albergo Pagano is a German who does nothing but go about hunting lizards; he shuts them up in a cigar-box, which he opens every now and then to gaze like another Gulliver upon his Lilliputian captives. We are deadly enemies, he and I, for once I opened his cigar-box and set all his lizards free.

Suddenly Puck gave a growl. We looked up, and to our great astonishment we saw two ladies standing in front of us, and behind them stood a gentleman in black, staring fixedly into space. We had not heard them come up, so that they must have been standing there while D——— and I were busy finishing off the commercial traveller's poem. We looked at each other in consternation, but there was evidently nothing to fear; it was not difficult to see that they were English, and not likely to have understood one word of what we had been talking about. One of the ladies was middle-aged, rather stout, and wore a gray travelling-dress, while the other was a very smart young lady, whom we thought very good-looking indeed. They stood there gazing out over the Marina, and on looking in the same direction we saw that the Princess's steamer had returned from its *giro* round the island, and had anchored beside the Naples boat. Our discomfiture was complete upon the younger of the ladies turning round to ask us in perfect French how long it would take them to get to the village. D——, who was lying nearest them, answered it would hardly take ten minutes.

"Is it necessary to go through the village in order to reach the beach?" said she, pointing towards the Marina.

"Yes," answered D——, "it is necessary to do so."

Here Puck stretched himself and stared yawningly at them.

"What a beautiful dog!" I heard the elder lady say to her companion in English. I at once discovered her to be a lady of great distinction and exceptional taste, and I immediately felt a desire to show her some politeness. I could not hit upon anything better to tell her than that she had chosen an unfortunate day for coming to Capri, the island having fallen a prey to the barbarians for the whole day. I told her that the Crown Princess of Germany was actually on the island, and that, pursued by a deputation and a commercial traveller, she had just now been caught on the Piccola Marina and carried off to the Piazza. I added that all our sympathies followed the Princess. I noticed a rather peculiar expression on the younger lady's face as I delivered myself of these remarks, but the elder listened to all I said with a scarcely perceptible smile over her eyes.

"We are anxious to reach the harbour as soon as possible," said she; "we have been absent longer than we intended."

"There is a short cut down to the Marina," answered I, politely; "we have just come up that way ourselves. But I am afraid it is rather too rough a road for you, madam."

"Will it lead us straight down there?" said she, pointing to the harbour where both steamers lay at anchor.

"Oh dear, yes!"

"And without obliging us to enter the village?"

"Without obliging you to enter the village," answered I.

She exchanged a few words with the younger lady, and then said in a decided, abrupt sort of way, "Be kind enough to show us the way."

Yes, that was easy enough, and I led them down to the Marina. Conversation rather languished on the way. I had come across two singularly reticent ladies, and had it not been for my repeated efforts it would have died altogether. Every now and then the younger lady smiled to herself, which made me fear I had said something stupid. I have never been much of a society man, and it is not so easy a matter to entertain two entirely strange ladies.

Upon reaching the wider part of the road I pointed towards the Marina at their feet, and told them that they could not possibly go wrong now. We saw one or two officers walking up and down the landing-stage, whereupon I told the ladies that, were they desirous of seeing the Crown Princess, they had only to wait there a moment or two; she was bound to arrive soon with her tormentors at her heels. But this, they said, they did not care about, and then they kindly wished me good-bye.

Hardly had I begun to retrace my steps when two lackeys in the royal livery of the house of Savoy came running down the road; I had barely time to move to one side before they were yards beyond me. They were immediately followed by a long, gaunt individual with very thin legs and a very big moustache—*ma foi!* if not a German officer, remarkably like one at all events. He in his turn was succeeded by a fat, fussy little person, who literally threw himself into my arms; he held his gold-laced hat in one hand, while with the other he wiped the perspiration from his forehead; he stammered an apology, and then rolled off again like a ball down the hill. Most extraordinary, thought I to myself, the number of people on this footpath to-day, considering that as a rule one never meets a soul here!

D—— still lay on the Anacapri road waiting for me; neither of us cared to return to Capri just then, and we finally made up our minds to walk up to Anacapri and greet la bella Margherita, and wait there till the island should be restored to calm. We sat for a while under the pergola and drank a glass of vino bianco, and then we slowly sauntered down to Capri along the beautiful road, the whole of the myrtle-covered mountain slope at our feet. When passing beneath Barbarossa's ruined castle we glanced towards the Marina and saw to our relief that both steamers had taken their departure. Genuine Capriotes always witness the departure of the steamer with a certain satisfaction; they like to keep their beloved Capri to themselves, and the crowd of noisy strangers only disturbs the harmony of the dreamy little island.

It was very nearly dark by the time we reached the village. The piazza was quite deserted; from the shop-window of Nicolino, barber and bleeder, hung the tricoloured flag waving sadly in the wind, whilst perched upon the triumphal arch the cardboard eagle sat aloft gnawing gloomily at his *Willkommen*.

Upon reaching the hotel we found that every one was seated at table, but an unusual silence prevailed. We withdrew to our little table and tried to look as innocent as possible. At dessert there arose a frightful dispute at the big table as to whose was the fault of a certain calamity which apparently had happened to them during the day. I thought I heard a murmur going round about an idiot who had been seen accompanying two ladies down a short cut to the Marina, but I never got to know who he was. Ah well! neither D——— nor I care to tell you more about this story. If we behaved badly I have already been sufficiently punished. Here I sit far from my beloved island in fog and gloom, whilst the commercial traveller, for aught I know, is perhaps still enjoying himself at Capri, and still entertaining the cocks of Pagano with—

"Ich stehe hier auf Felsenstrand!"

MENAGERIE

For a few days only!!!

BRUTUS, Lion from Nubia.

TIGERS, BEARS, WOLVES.

POLAR BEAR.

MONKEYS, HYÆNAS, and other remarkable
Animals.

The Lion-Tamer, called "THE LION KING,"
will enter the Lion's Cage at 6 o'clock.

For a few days only!!!

The street boys hold out for a while longer, cold though the evening be, for the Lion King himself has already twice appeared on the platform in riding-boots, and his breast sparkling with decorations, and, besides that, one can distinctly hear the howling of the animals within the tent.

Yes, it would be a pity to miss an entertainment like this; come, let us go in!

It is the Lion King's wife herself who is sitting there selling the tickets, and we gaze at her with a deference due to her rank. She wears gold bracelets round her thick wrists, and a double gold chain glitters beneath her fur cape. But the monkeys who sit there on each side of her chained to their perches with leather straps girt tightly round their stomachs—they wear no fur capes. Their faces are blue with cold, and when they jump up and down to try to keep themselves warm the street boys laugh and the market people stop to have a look at them—poor unconscious clowns of the menagerie who are there for the purpose of luring in spectators to witness the tortures of their other companions in distress.

The tent is full of people, and the many gas-lights inflame the infected air. The show has already begun, and the spectators follow from cage to cage a negro, who, pointing his stick at the prisoner behind the bars, in monotonous voice announces his age, his country, and his crime of having led the life which Nature has taught him to live.

I have been here several times, and I know the negro's description by heart. I will show you the animals.

Here, in this cage, moping on his perch, his head hidden beneath his ragged feather-cloak, you see the proudest representative of the bird world—*The Royal Eagle, three years old, taken young.* You have read about him, the strong-winged bird, who in solemn majesty circles above the desolate mountain-tops. Alone he lives up there amongst the clouds—alone like the human soul. He builds his nest upon an inaccessible rock, and the precipice shields his young from rapacious hands. *Taken young;* that means that the nest was plundered, the mother was shot as she flew shrieking to protect her child, and by the butt-end of the gun was broken the wing-bone of the half-grown eagle as he struggled for his freedom. Here he has sat ever since; he sleeps during the day, but he is awake the live-long night, and when all is silent in the tent a strange, uncanny moan may be heard from his cage. *Three years old!* He is not the most to be pitied here, for he is not likely to last long—the Royal Eagle dies when caged.

Here you see a *Bear.* His cage is so small that he cannot walk up and down; he sits there almost upright on his hindquarters, rocking his meek and heavy head from side to side. If you offer him a piece of bread, he flattens his nose against the bars and gently and carefully takes the gift out of your hand. His nose is torn by the iron ring he once was made to wear, and his eyes are bloodshot and streaming from the strong gaslight; but their expression is not bad, it is kind and intelligent like that of an old dog. Now and then he grips the bars with his mighty paws, helplessly shaking the cage until the guinea-pigs who live below him rush up and down in abject terror. Ay, shake your cage, old Bruin! the bars are steel, stronger than your paws; you will never come out—you are to die in your prison. You are a dangerous beast of prey—you live on bilberries and fruit, and now and then you help yourself to a sheep to keep yourself from dying of starvation. God Almighty did not know better than to teach you to do so, but no doubt it was very ill-judged of Him, and you are very much to blame; it is only man who has the right to eat his fill.

Here you see a *Hyæna.* The negro stirs up the hyæna with a cut of his whip, and timorously the animal crouches in the farthermost corner of the cage, whilst the negro tells the spectators that the hyæna is known for its cowardice. The hyæna dare not risk an open fight, but treacherously attacks the defenceless prisoner whom the savages have left bound hand and foot to his fate in the wilderness, or the exhausted beast of burden whom the caravan has abandoned in the desert after having hoisted on to another the load he is no longer able to bear. The negro pokes cautiously with his pointed stick into the corner where the cowardly animal tries to hide itself, and the spectators all agree that the hyæna, with its crouching back and restless eyes, conveys a faithful picture of treachery and cowardice. None of the spectators have ever seen a hyæna before, but they have seen crouching backs and restless eyes. Not even the dead does the hyæna leave in peace, says the negro, and with disgust man turns away from the guilty animal.

Here you see a *Polar Bear*. Its name is advertised in huge letters on the placard outside; and he deserves the distinction well indeed, for his torture perhaps surpasses that of all the other animals. The Polar bear is another dangerous beast of prey; he does a little fishing for himself up in the north where man is busy exterminating the whales. The horrible sufferings of the animal need no comment—let us go on.

A little *South African Monkey* and a rabbit live next to the cage inhabited by the panting Polar bear.[13]

The little monkey is sick to death of the eternal clambering up and down the bars of the cage, and the swing which dangles over her head does not amuse her any more. Sadly she sits there upon her straw-covered prison floor, in one hand she holds a half-withered carrot, which she turns over once again to see if it looks equally unappetising on every side, while with the other she sorrowfully scratches the rabbit's back. Now and then she gets interested, drops the carrot, and attentively with both hands explores some suspicious-looking spot on her companion's mangy back and pulls out a few hairs, which she carefully examines. But soon she wearies of the rabbit also, and does not know in the least what to do with herself. She looks round in the straw, but there is nothing to be seen but the carrot; she looks round the bare, slippery walls of her cage, but neither there is there anything of the slightest interest to be found. And at last she has nothing else to do but, for the hundredth time that hour, to jump into the swing, only to leap on to the floor the next minute and seat herself again, leaning against the rabbit. The spectators call this jumping for joy, but the poor little monkey knows how jolly it is.

The rabbit is resigned. The captivity of generations has stupefied him—the longing for liberty has died ages ago from out of his degenerated hare-brain. He hopes for nothing, but he desires nothing. He has no social talents; he is in no way qualified to entertain his restless friend; and besides that, he fails to grasp the situation. But he rewards the monkey to the best of his abilities for the little offices of friendship which she performs for him; and when the gas has been turned out, and the cold night air enters the tent, then the Northerner lends his warm fur coat to the trembling little Southerner, and nestling close to one another they await the new day.

The inhabitant of the cage in yonder corner has not been advertised at all upon the placard outside. He is not to be seen just now; perhaps he is asleep for a while in his dark, little bedroom; but every one who catches sight of that wire wheel knows that it is a *Squirrel* who lives here. What he has to do in a menagerie is more than I can say, for on that point the zoological education of the public should surely be completed—we all know what the squirrel looks like. Superstitious people of my country say that it is an evil omen if a squirrel crosses their path. I don't know where they got hold of that idea, but maybe they have taken it from a squirrel—for the squirrel believes exactly in the same way if a man crosses his path, and, alas! he has got reason enough for his belief. I, on the contrary, have always thought it a piece of good luck whenever I have happened to come across a little squirrel. Often enough while roaming through the woods and halting with grateful joy at every other step before some new wonder in the fairyland of nature— often enough have I caught a glimpse of the graceful, nimble, little fellow swinging himself high overhead on some leafy branch, or carefully peeping out from his little twig cottage, watching with his bright eyes whether any schoolboys were lurking beneath his tree. "Come along, little man," I then would say in squirrel language; "true enough, I did not turn out the man I had been expected to become when at school; but, thank God! I have at least arrived so far in knowledge that I have learned to feel tender sympathy for you and yours!" We were, alas! not taught this at school in my days; we exchanged birds' eggs for old stamps; we shot small birds with guns as big as ourselves—and now let him who can come and deny the doctrine of original sin! We were cruel to animals, like all savages. To the best of my abilities do I now endeavour to expiate the wrong I was then guilty of. But an evil action never dies; and I know of bloodstains on tiny boys' fingers which have rusted to stains of shame in the childhood recollections of the man. To my humiliation I have shot many a little bird, and many another did I keep imprisoned. Regretfully do I also own to having killed a squirrel; treacherously did I plunder his home, and his little one did I imprison in just such another cage as the one we now stand in front of. See! there comes the little squirrel out from his bedroom and begins to run round and round in his wire wheel. He has made the same attempt thousands and thousands of times, and yet he makes it once again. Yes, it looks very pretty! when I used to watch my squirrel running round and round in his wire wheel in precisely the same way, and at last the wheel was turning so rapidly that I could not distinguish the bars, I thought it was capital fun. I know now why he runs; he runs in anxious longing for freedom; he runs as long as he has strength to run; for neither is *he* able to distinguish any more the bars of the turning wheel. He may run a mile and still he is hedged in by the same prison bars. The simple invention is almost diabolically cunning; it is the wheel of Ixion in the Tartarus of pain to which mankind has banished animals.

Here you see a *Wolf from Siberia*. The wolf is also, as is well known, a dangerous, wild beast. When the cold is extreme, and the snow lies very deep, the wolves approach the habitation of man, and in starving crowds they follow any sledge they meet—they have even been known in very rare cases to attack the horses. We have all read that terrible story of the Russian peasant on his way home across the deserted snow-fields; he heard the panting of the wolves behind his sledge, and he could see their eyes glitter through the darkness of the night, and in order to save his own life he had to throw one of his children to the wolves.

The negro informs you that the wild beast in this cage was caught young; the she-wolf as usual was killed while attempting to save her cub.

The bottom of the cage is shining like a parquet floor from the continual tramping up and down of the prisoner within, for he knows no rest. Night and day he paces to and fro, his head bent low as though in search of some outlet of escape; he will never find it; he will die behind those bars even as the prisoners in his own country die in their irons.

The big *Parrot* on her perch over there sheds the one ray of light on this dark picture. The parrot I need not describe to you, for you know the species well. This one hails, we are told, from the New World, but one comes across a good many parrots in the Old World also. The parrot is a universal favourite and is to be found in nearly every house. The parrot is not unhappy; she is unconscious of the chain round her leg, she does not realise that she was born with wings. She is undisturbed by any unnecessary brain activity; she eats, she sleeps, trims her gorgeous feather cloak, and chatters ceaselessly from morning till night. Left to herself she is silent, for she is only able to repeat what others have said before her, and this she does so cleverly that often, on hearing some one chatter, I have to ask myself whether it be a human being or a parrot. . . .

The ragged, attenuated animal standing over there and gazing at us with her soft, sad eyes is a *Chamois from Switzerland*. The chamois is a rarity in a menagerie, for, as is well known, it usually frets to death during the first year of its captivity. I look at the poor animal with a feeling of oppression at my heart which you can scarcely realise—I have breathed the free air of the high mountains myself, and I know why the chamois dies in prison. Those were other times, poor captive chamois, when you were roving on the Alpine meadows amidst rhododendrons and myrtillus; when on high, over a precipice, I saw your beautiful silhouette standing out against the clear, bright sky! You had no need of an alpenstock, you, to climb up there, where I watched the aerial play of your graceful limbs amongst the rocks. Up to the realm of ice you led the way, high on the slopes of Monte Rosa has my clumsy, human foot trodden the snow in the track of your dainty mountain shoes. Ay, those were other times, poor prisoner!—those were other times both for you and me, and we had better say no more about them.

Yonder stalwart, muscular ape is a *Baboon; aged, Abyssinian male*, stands written under his cage. He sits there, wrapped in thought, fingering a straw. Now and then he casts a rapid glance around him, and be sure he is not so absent-minded as he looks. The eye is intelligent but malevolent; its owner is a candidate for humanity.

When the negro approaches his cage he shows him a row of teeth not very unlike the negro's own—the family likeness between the two faces is, for the matter of that, unmistakable. The negro cautions the public against accepting the wrinkled hand which the old baboon extends between the bars. I always treat him to an extra lump of sugar ever since the negro told me he once bit off the thumb of an old woman who poked her umbrella at him. Besides, I look at him with veneration, for he comes from an illustrious family. Who knows whether he is not an ill-starred descendant of that heroic old baboon whom Brehm once met in Abyssinia?—The negro is sure to know nothing of that story, so I may as well tell it you. One day, while travelling in Abyssinia, the great German naturalist fell in with a whole troop of baboons, who, bound for some high rocks, were marching along a narrow defile. The rear had not yet emerged from the defile when the dogs of Brehm and his companions rushed forward and barred their passage. Seeing the danger the other baboons, who had already reached the rocks, then descended in a body to the rescue of the attacked, and they screamed so terribly that the dogs actually fell back; the whole troop of baboons was now filing off in perfect order when the dogs were again set at them. All the apes, however, reached the rocks in safety, with the exception of one half-year-old baboon who happened to have been lagging behind; he was surrounded on all sides by the open-mouthed dogs, and with loud cries of distress he jumped on to a big boulder. At this juncture a huge baboon stepped down from the rocks for the second time, advanced alone to the stone where the little one was crouching, patted him on the back, lifted him gently down, and so led him off triumphantly before the very noses of the dogs, who were so taken by surprise that it never even occurred to them to attack him. One need not have read Darwin to pronounce that baboon a hero.

I have noticed that even kind-hearted spectators do not seem to feel very much commiseration for captive monkeys. The ape is playing in the menagerie the same rôle as Don Quixote in literature—the superficial observer looks upon them as exclusively comical, and only laughs at them. But the attentive looker-on knows that the solitary monkey's life behind the bars is in its way nothing but a tragedy, as well as Cervantes' immortal book is nothing but a mournful epic. With tender emotion he feels how an increasing sympathy mingles in his pitiful smile the more he gets to know of them, these two superannuated types: Don Quixote, the simple-minded, would-be hero, still lagging on the scene long after the *epopée* of chivalry has departed in the twilight of mediæval mysticism; and the ape, the phantom from the vanishing animal world, over whose hairy human face already falls the dawn of the birthday of the first man.

This baboon may perhaps appear to you very ugly, but we know that the perception of physical beauty is an entirely individual one, and it is quite possible that the baboon on his side finds us very ugly. You cannot help smiling now and then when standing and watching him, but, at least, try not to let him see it, for, like all monkeys, it saddens and irritates him to be laughed at to his face. This old baboon is deeply unhappy, for, as he has got more brains than the other animals in the menagerie, his capacity for suffering is consequently greater—for we all know that suffering is an intellectual function. He alone realises the hopelessness of his situation, and his restless brain-activity refuses him the relative oblivion which resignation vouchsafes to many others of his companions in distress.

But as a compensation he possesses one quality which the other animals lack, and it is the possession of this quality which saves him from falling into hypochondria;—it is his sense of humour. That the monkey is a born humorist every one knows who has had the opportunity of observing him in society—for instance, in the monkey-house at the Zoo. This sense of humour does not even desert the poor monkey kept in solitary confinement. And sometimes when I have been standing here for a while watching the mimicry of this old baboon I have involuntarily had to ask myself whether he were not making fun of me. . . .

The negro has finished his recital, and it is time for the show-piece of the evening to come off. The spectators crowd in front of the lion-cage, dividing their admiration between Brutus, the Nubian lion, behind the bars and the keeper who, unarmed, is about to enter the cage. The man throws off his overcoat and the "Lion King" stands before us in all his pride, pink tights, riding-boots, and his gold-laced breast covered with decorations—from Nubia likewise even these. He is small of stature like Napoleon, and the constant intercourse with the wild beasts has given his face a rough and repulsive expression. He reeks of brandy, to counteract the stale smell of the cage, and his pomatumed hair curls neatly round his low-sloping forehead. The negro hands him a whip, and the solemn moment is at hand. Proudly the Lion King creeps into the cage, and proudly he cracks his whip at the half-sleeping Brutus. The lion raises himself with a sullen roar, and, hugging the walls, begins to wander round his cage. Proudly the Lion King stretches out his whip, and obediently like a dog Brutus leaps lazily over it. Proudly the negro hands his master a hoop, and wearily and dejectedly Brutus jumps through it. Brutus is sulky to-night; he does not roar as he ought to do. Things look up, however, towards the end of the performance, when the Lion King, standing in a corner of the cage, paralyses Brutus with a proud look just as he is about to attack him. Brutus is no longer obstinate, but roars irreproachably, and shows his yellow fang. A few half-smothered cries of alarm are heard from the audience, an old woman faints, a pistol is fired off while the Lion King, under cover of the smoke, hurriedly and proudly creeps out of the cage.

Captive lion, have you then forgotten that once you were a king yourself, that once there was a time when all men trembled at your approach, that the forest grew silent when your imperious voice resounded? Fallen monarch, awake from the degradation of your thraldom; rise giant-like and let the thunder of your royal voice be heard once more!

Brutus, Brutus, vindicator of lost freedom, you are too proud to be a slave! Rend asunder the chains which coward human cunning has bound around the sleeping power of your limbs!

Shake your flaming lion mane, and, strong as Samson, in your mighty wrath bring down the prison walls around you to crush the Philistines assembled here to jeer at the impotence of their once dreaded enemy!

Brutus, Brutus, vindicator of lost freedom!

ITALY IN PARIS

At one time I had many patients in the Roussel Yard. Ten or twelve families lived there, but none were so badly off, I believe, as the Salvatore family. At Salvatore's it was so dark that they were obliged to burn a little oil-lamp the whole day, and there was no fireplace except a brazier which stood in the middle of the floor. Damp as a cellar it was at all times; but when it rained the water penetrated into the room, which lay a couple of feet lower than the street.

And nevertheless one could see in everything a kind of pathetic struggle against the gloomy impression which the dwelling itself made. Old illustrated papers were pasted up round the walls, the bed was neat and clean, and behind an old curtain in one corner, the family's little wardrobe was hung up in the neatest order. Salvatore himself, with skilful hand, had made the little girl's bed out of an old box, and in the day one could sit upon it as if it were a sofa. The corner shelf where the Madonna stood was adorned with bright-coloured paper flowers, and there, too, the small treasures of the family lay spread out,—the gilt brooch which Salvatore had presented to his wife when they were married; the string of corals which her brother had brought from the coral fishery in "Barbaria" (Algeria); the two gorgeous cups out of which coffee was drunk on solemn occasions; and there, too, stood the wonderful porcelain dog which Concetta had once received as a present from a grand lady, and which was only taken down on Sundays to be admired more closely.

I did not understand how the mother managed it; but the little girls were always neat and tidy in their outgrown clothes, and their faces shone, so washed and polished were they. The eldest child, Concetta, had been at the free school for more than half a year; and it was the mother's pride to make her read aloud to me out of her book. She herself had never learned to read, and although I allowed myself to be told that Salvatore read very well, neither he nor I had ever ventured to try his capabilities. Now, since Petruccio could hardly ever get out of bed, Concetta had been obliged to give up going to school, so that she might stay at home with her sick brother whilst *la mamma* was at her work away in the eating-house. This place could not be given up, as not only did she get ten sous a day for washing dishes, but sometimes she could bring home scraps under her apron, which no one else could turn to account, but out of which she managed to make a capital soup for Petruccio.

Salvatore himself worked the whole day away in La Villette. He was obliged to be at the stone-mason's yard at six o'clock every morning, and it was much too far to go home during the mid-day rest. Sometimes it happened that I was there when he came home in the evening after his day's work, and then he looked very proudly at me when Petruccio stretched out his arms towards him. He took his little son up so carefully with his big horny hands, lifted him on his broad shoulders, and tenderly leaned his sunburnt cheek against the sick little one's waxen face. Petruccio sat quite quiet and silent on his father's arm; sometimes he laid hold of his father's matted beard with his thin fingers, and then Salvatore looked very happy. "*Vedete, Signor dottore*," he then would say, "*n'è vero che sta meglio sta sera?*"[14] He received his week's wages every Saturday, and then he always came home triumphantly with a little toy for his son, and both father and mother knelt down beside the bed to see how Petruccio liked it. Petruccio, alas! liked scarcely anything. He took the toy in his hand, but that was all. Petruccio's face was old and withered, and his solemn, weary eyes were not the eyes of a child. I had never known him cry or complain, but neither had I seen him smile except once when he was given a great hairy horse—a horse which stretched out its tongue when one turned it upside down. But it was not every day that a horse like that could be got.

Petruccio was four years old, but he could not speak. He would lie hour after hour quite quiet and silent, but he did not sleep: his great eyes stood wide open, and it seemed as if he saw something far beyond the narrow walls of the room—"*Sta sempre in pensiero*,"[15] said Salvatore.

Petruccio was supposed to understand everything which was said around him, and nothing of importance was undertaken in the little family without first trying to discover Petruccio's opinion of the affair; and if any one believed that they could read disapproval in the features of the soulless little one, the whole question fell to the ground at once, and it was afterwards found that Petruccio had almost always been right.

On Sundays Salvatore sat at home, and there were usually some other holiday-dressed workmen visiting him, and in low-toned voices they sat and argued about wages, about news from *il paese*, and sometimes Salvatore treated them to a litre of wine, and they played a game, *alla scopa*. Sometimes it was supposed that Petruccio wished to look on, and then his little bed was moved to the bench where they sat; and sometimes Petruccio wished to be alone, and then Salvatore and his guests moved out into the passage. I had, however, remarked that Petruccio's wish to be alone, and the consequent removal of the company to the passage, usually happened when the wife was away: if she were at home she saw plainly that Petruccio wished his father to stay indoors and not go out with the others. And Petruccio was right enough there, too. Salvatore was not very difficult to persuade if one of the guests wished to treat him in his turn. Once out in the passage, it happened often enough that he went off to the wine-shop too. And once there, it was not so easy for Salvatore to get away again.

What was still more difficult was the coming home. His wife forgave him certainly,—she had done it so many times before; but Salvatore knew that Petruccio was inexorable, and the thicker the mist of intoxication fell over him, the more crushed did he feel himself under Petruccio's reproachful eye. No dissimulation helped here; Petruccio saw through it at once. Petruccio could even see how much he had drunk, as Salvatore himself confided to me one Sunday evening when I came upon him sitting out in the passage, in the deepest repentance. Salvatore was, alas! obviously uncertain in his speech that evening, and it did not need Petruccio's perspicacity to see that he had drunk more than usual. I asked him if he would not go in, but he wished to remain outside to get *un poco d'aria*; he was, however, very anxious to know if Petruccio were awake or not, and I promised to come out and tell him. I also thought it was best he should sit out there till his head should clear itself a little bit, though not so much for Petruccio's sake as to spare his wife; and for that matter this was not the first time I had been Salvatore's confidant in the like difficult situation. They who see the lives of the poor near at hand cannot be very severe upon a working man who, after he has toiled twelve hours a day the whole week, sometimes gets a little wine into his head. It is a melancholy fact, but we must judge it leniently; for we must not forget that here at least society has hardly offered the poorer classes any other distraction.

I therefore advised my friend Salvatore to sit outside till I came back, and I went in alone. Inside sat the wife with her child of sorrow in her arms; and the even breathing of the little girls could be heard from the box. Petruccio was supposed to know me very well, and even to be fond of me—although he had never shown it in any way, nor, as far as I knew, had any sort of feeling ever been mirrored in his face. The mother's eye, so clear-sighted in everything, nevertheless did not see that there was no soul in the child's vacant eye; the mother's ear, so sensible to each breath of the little one, yet did not hear that the confused sounds which sometimes came from his lips would never form themselves into human speech. Petruccio had been ill from his birth, his body was shrunken, and no thought lived under the child's wrinkled forehead. Unhappily I could do nothing for him; all I could hope for was that the ill-favoured little one should soon die. And it looked as if his release were near. That Petruccio had been worse for some time both the mother and I had understood; and this evening he was so feeble that he was not able to hold his head up. Petruccio had refused all food since yesterday, and Salvatore's wife, when I came in, was just trying to persuade him, with all the sweet words which only a mother knows, to swallow a little milk; but he would not. In vain the mother put the spoon to his mouth and said that it was wonderfully good, in vain did she appeal to my presence, "*Per fare piacere al Signor dottore*,"—Petruccio would not. His forehead was puckered, and his eyes had a look of painful anxiety, but no complaint came from his tightly compressed lips.

Suddenly the mother gave a scream. Petruccio's face was distorted with cramp, and a strong convulsion shook his whole little body. The attack was soon over; and whilst Petruccio was being laid in his bed, I tried to calm the mother as well as I could by telling her that children often had convulsions which were of very little importance, and that there was no further danger from this one now. I looked up and I saw Salvatore, who stood leaning against the door-post. He had taken courage, and had staggered to the door, and, unseen by us, he had witnessed that sight so terrifying to unaccustomed eyes. He was pale as a corpse, and great tears ran down the cheeks which had been so lately flushed with drink. "*Castigo di Dio! Castigo di Dio!*"[16] muttered he with trembling voice; and he fell on his knees by the door, as if he dared not approach the feeble cripple who seemed to him like God's mighty avenger.

The unconscious little son had once more shown his father the right way; Salvatore went no more to the wine-shop.

Petruccio grew worse and worse, and the mother no longer left his side. And it was scarcely a month after she lost her place that Salvatore's accident happened: he fell from a scaffolding and broke his leg. He was taken to the Lariboisière Hospital; and the company for whom he worked paid fifty centimes a day to his family, which they were not obliged to do,—so that Salvatore's wife had to be very grateful for it. Every Thursday—the visiting day at the hospital—she was with him for an hour; and I too saw him now and then. The days went on, and with Petruccio's mother want increased more and more. The porcelain dog stood alone now on the Madonna's shelf; and it was not long before the holiday clothes went the same way as the treasures—to the pawnshop. Petruccio needed broth and milk every day, and he had them. The little girls too had enough, I believe, to satisfy them more or less; but what the mother herself lived upon I do not know.

I had already tried many times to take Petruccio to the children's hospital, where he would have been much better off, but as usual all my powers of eloquence could not achieve this: the poor, as is well known, will hardly ever be separated from their sick children. The lower middle class and the town artisans have learnt to understand the value of the hospital, but the really poor mother, whose culture is very low, will not leave the side of her sick child: the exceptions to this rule are extremely rare.

And so came the 15th, the dreaded day when the quarter's rent must be paid, when the working man drags his mattress to the pawn-shop, and the wife draws off her ring, which in her class means much more than in ours; the day full of terror, when numberless suppliants stand with lowered heads before their landlord, and when hundreds of families do not know where they will sleep the next night.

I happened to pass by there on that very evening, and at the door stood Salvatore's little girl crying all to herself. I asked her why she cried, but that she did not know; at last, however, I learned that she cried because "*la mamma piange tanto*."[17] Inside the yard I ran against my friend Archangelo Fusco, the street-sweeper, who lived next door to the Salvatores. He was occupied in dragging his bed out into the yard, and I did not need to wait for his explanation to understand that he had been evicted.[18] I asked him where he was going to move to, and he hoped to sleep that night at the Refuge in the Rue Tocqueville, and afterwards he must find out some other place. Inside sat Salvatore's wife crying by Petruccio's bed, and on the table stood a bundle containing the clothes of the family. The Salvatore family had not been able to pay their rent, and the Salvatore family had been evicted. The landlord had been there that afternoon, and had said that the room was let from the morning of the next day. I asked her where she thought of going, and she said she did not know.

I had often heard the dreaded landlord talked of; the year before I had witnessed the same sorrowful scene, when he had turned out into the street a couple of unhappy families and laid hands upon the little they possessed. I had never seen him personally, but I thought it might be useful in my study of human nature to make his acquaintance. Archangelo Fusco offered to take me to him, and we set forth slowly. On the way my companion informed me that the landlord was "*molto ricco*"; besides the whole court he owned a large house in the vicinity, and this did not surprise me in the least, because I had long known that he secretly carried on that most lucrative of all professions—money-lending to the poor. Archangelo Fusco considered that he on his side had nothing to gain by a meeting with the landlord, and after he had told me that besides the rent he also owed him ten francs, we agreed that he should only accompany me to the entrance.

A shabbily-dressed old man, with a bloated, disagreeable face opened the door carefully, and after he had looked me over, admitted me into the room. I mentioned my errand, and asked him to allow Salvatore to settle his rent in a few days' time. I told him that Salvatore himself lay in the hospital, that the child was dying, and that his severity towards these poor people was inhuman cruelty. He asked who I was, and I answered that I was a friend of the family. He looked at me, and with an ugly laugh he said that I could best show that by at once paying their rent. I felt the blood rushing to my head, I hope and believe it was only with anger, for one never ought to blush because one is not rich. I listened for a couple of minutes whilst he abused my poor destitute Italians with the coarsest words; he said that they were a dirty thieving pack, who did not deserve to be treated like human beings; that Salvatore drank up his wages; that the street-sweeper had stolen ten francs from him; and that they all of them well deserved the misery in which they lived.

I asked if he needed this money just now, and from his answer I understood that here no prayers would avail. He was rich; he owned over 50,000 francs in money, he said, and he had begun with nothing of his own. It is a melancholy fact that the man who has risen from destitution to riches is usually cruel to the poor: one would hope and believe the contrary, but this is unhappily the case.

My intention when I went there was to endeavour with diplomatic cunning to effect a kind of arrangement, but alas! I was not the man for that. I lost my temper altogether and went further than I had intended to do, as usual. At first he answered me scornfully and with coarse insults, but he soon grew silent, and I ended by talking alone I should say for nearly an hour's time. It would serve no purpose to relate what I said to him; there are occasions when it is legitimate to show one's anger in action, but it is always stupid to show it in words. I said to him, however, that this money which had been squeezed out of the poor was the wages of sin; that his debt to all these poor human beings was far greater than theirs to him. I pointed to the crucifix which hung against the wall, and I said that if any divine justice was to be found on this earth, vengeance could not fail to reach him, and that no prayers could buy his deliverance from the punishment which awaited him, for his life was stained with the greatest of all sins—namely cruelty towards the poor. "And take care, old blood-sucker!" I shouted out at last with threatening voice; "You owe your money to the poor, but you owe yourself to the devil, and the hour is near when he will demand his own again!" I checked myself, startled, for the man sank down in his chair as if touched by an unseen hand, and pale as death, he stared at me with a terror which I felt communicated itself to me. The curse I had just called down rang still in my ears with a strange uncanny sound, which I did not recognise; and it seemed to me as if there were some one else in the room besides us two.

I was so agitated that I have no recollection of how I came away. When I got home it was already late, but I did not sleep a wink all night; and even to this day I think with wonder of the waking dream which that night filled me with an inconceivable emotion. I dreamt that I had condemned a man to death.

When I got there in the forenoon the blow had already fallen upon me. I *knew* what had happened although no human being had told me. All the inhabitants of the yard were assembled before the door in eager talk. "*Sapete Signor dottore?*"[19] they called out as soon as they saw me.

"Yes, I know," answered I, and hurried to Salvatore's. I bent down over Petruccio and pretended to examine his chest; but breathless I listened to every word that the wife said to me.

The landlord had come down there late yesterday evening, she said. The little girl had run away and hidden herself when he came into the room; but Concetta had remained behind her mother's chair, and when he asked why they were so afraid of him, Concetta had answered because he was so cruel to mamma. He had sat there upon the bench a long time without saying a word, but he did not look angry, Salvatore's wife thought. At last he said to her she need not be anxious about the rent; she could wait to pay it till next time. And when he left he laid a five-franc piece upon the table to buy something for Petruccio. Outside the door he had met Archangelo Fusco with his bed on a hand-cart, preparing to take himself off, and he had told the street-sweeper too that he could remain in his lodging. He had asked Archangelo Fusco about me, and Archangelo Fusco, who judged me with friendship's all-forgiving forbearance, had said nothing unkind about me. He had then gone on his way, and according to what was discovered by the police investigations he had, contrary to his habit, passed the evening in the wine-shop close by, and the porter had thought he looked drunk when he came home. As he lived quite alone, and for fear of thieves or from avarice, attended to his housekeeping himself, no one knew what had happened; but lights were burning in the house the whole night, and when he did not come down in the morning, and his door was fastened inside, they had begun to suspect foul play and sent for the police. He was still warm when they cut him down; but the doctor whom the police sent for said that he had already been dead a couple of hours. They had not been able to discover the smallest reason for his hanging himself. All that was known was that he had been visited in the evening by a strange gentleman who had stayed with him more than an hour, and the neighbours had heard a violent dispute going on inside. No one in the house had seen the strange gentleman before, and no one knew who he was.

The Roussel Yard belongs now to the dead man's brother; and to my joy the new landlord's first action was to have the rooms in it repaired, so that now they look more habitable. He also lowered the rents.

The Salvatores moved thence when Petruccio died; but the place is still full of Italians. I go there now and then; and in spite of all the talk about the Paris doctors' *jalousie de métier*, I have never yet met any one who tried to supplant me in this practice.

BLACKCOCK-SHOOTING

The passion for the chase is man's passion for pursuing, and if possible killing, animals living in liberty. The passion for the chase is the expression of the same impulse of the stronger to overthrow the weaker which goes through the whole animal series. The wild beast's lust for murder has been tamed to unconscious instinct, and thousand years of culture lie between our wild ancestors who slew each other with stone axes for a piece of raw fish, and the sportsman of our day. But it is only the method which has been refined, the principle is the same.

The passion for killing is an animal instinct, and as such, impossible to eradicate. But it behoves man, conscious of his high rank, to struggle against this vice of his wild childhood, this phantom from the grave in which sleep the progenitors of his race.

I cannot give you here in detail my proposals for new game laws—the matter is not yet quite ripe—but I am very willing to explain the fundamental principle on which they rest. I maintain that the very great start which mankind has gained through the law of natural selection has made the struggle between the man and the animal *too unequal to be fair*; I maintain that killing animals is an unmanly and an ignoble occupation.

Yes, but as regards wild beasts, wolves, foxes, etc., you don't really mean to stand up for them? Of course I do! First of all it has never been proved that the wild animals attacked man the first. And in the hopeless, defensive warfare in which the animals with vanishing strength struggle against mankind, all my sympathies are unhesitatingly given to the weaker. Yes, it is quite true that now and then they take a hen or a sheep from us; but what is that in comparison with all we take from them, from woods and fields which were meant to be their larder as well as ours? And do not talk too much about the ferocity of the wolf, you men, who have the heart treacherously to put out poisoned food for the starving animal! Perhaps you have not seen this way of killing wolves, but I have. I have seen the victim's agony written in the snow; seen how he has walked a little way and then begun to totter; has fallen, and with ebbing strength tried to get up again; in mad delirium has rolled in the snow whilst the poison was burning his bowels, and then at last has lain down to die. And I have watched the trapper when he joyfully came to seize his prey.

Do not talk too much about the cunning of the fox, you men who have invented the spring-traps which cut into his leg when he tries to take the lying bait which you have set out for him. In England you have not seen this way of catching foxes, but I have. I have seen the prisoner struggling with his last strength to get free, with the blood flowing from his wounded leg, cut to the bone by the sharp iron; I have heard the animal's moan far off in the night, and I have seen the footmarks in the snow of his comrades, who have anxiously roamed around.

"But this is horrible! how is it possible that such a thing can be allowed?"

"Yes, you are right; it is horrible; but this is the death which awaits many foxes both in Russia and Scandinavia, and in Germany too."

"In England it would be considered a crime to kill a fox in that way."

"Yes, I know well that England is the country for lovers of animals. What a fine graceful animal is the fox——"

"Only think what would become of the noblest of all sports, that of fox-hunting——"

Fox-hunting! and you call that a noble sport? I will tell you what fox-hunting is—no, I think I will not tell you. I will only say that were I a fox, I think I would rather try to cross the Channel and become a continental fox than to be hunted to death by your hounds and your spurred horses. And the spur which urges you on, what is that? The love of galloping away on a fiery horse in wild chase over hedge and ditch—ah! I understand that joy well! But why must you have an animal flying in terror for its life before you? Why not leave the pursuers and the pursued to themselves if the latter is doomed to die and has to die? Why do you wish to witness his desperate struggle for life against his manifold stronger enemy? And why, if everything be all right, do you often enough feel something akin to satisfaction if by chance the fox escapes? I only ask, I dare not answer—I dare not for fear of my Editor. And I think we had better drop this subject altogether; it is too dangerous a one to discuss before an English public.

Once when travelling in Norway I heard of a famous man, the wealthiest of that country. I was told he had made his fame and his money as a promoter of a new method of catching whales. Nature to protect the whales has given them their slippery coat and their thick lining of blubber, but that man has overreached Nature. He kills them with dynamite. You ask, as I did, when I heard the horrible story, if that man has not been hanged. Alas, my poor friend! we do not understand the world at all; the man has by no means been hanged. True that a cord has been put round his neck, but it was the cord of Commander of St. Olaf—*sapristi!* they are not very particular in that country! I am very sorry for him, but were I to meet that man I would decline to shake hands with him. What have the whales done to man to be treated in this way? Have they not always been inoffensive and harmless ever since that kind old whale who happened to swallow the prophet Jonah, and then spat him carefully back on the shore? Only think what a horrible idea to blast in pieces a sensitive body as one blasts in pieces a rock! Think what a barbarous conception of man's position towards animals is here allowed to be put in practice, think of that—before the man is promoted to a Grand Cross of his St. Olaf!

Before giving the last touches to my new game-laws—the fundamental principles of which I have hinted to you—I am perfectly willing to listen to any legitimate claims of the sportsman, and I shall be glad to try to satisfy them if they do not harm the animals. But on one point I am firm. Under no pretext shall children be allowed to shoot, on account of the great development this occupation gives to the instinctive cruelty of the child, and the rude colour it lends to the formation of the whole character. Kindness to our inferiors we ought to be taught as children; life will surely teach us to grow hard enough. Nor are children to be allowed to watch shooting; for men's faces turn so ugly when they are pursuing a flying animal, and the child should be protected as much as possible from the sight of anything unbeautiful.

Ah! I remember so well a little lad up in Sweden who had escaped from school one clear spring morning. He saw how the trees were budding and the meadows in flower, and high up in the air he heard the song of the first skylark. The boy lay down silently in the grass and listened with thankfulness and joy. He knew well what the skylark sang: it sang that the long winter was over, and that it was springtime in the North. And he stared at the little bird high up in the bright air; he stared at it till the tears came into his eyes. He would have liked to kiss the wings which had borne it far over the wide sea home again; he would have liked to warm it at his heart in the frosty spring nights; he would have liked to guard its summer nest from all evil. Yes, surely the skylark could have remained longer in the land of eternal summer! But it knew that up in the cold North there wandered about men longing for spring breezes and summer sun, for flowers and song of birds. So it flew home, the courageous little bird, home to the frozen field from where the pale morning sun melted the white frost-flowers of the night, where primroses and anemones were waking up from their winter sleep. With the head hidden under the down of its wings it kept out the cold of the night, and when the horizon brightened, it flew up and sang its joyful morning hymn—sang Nature's promise of life-bringing sun. But the next day the boy read in the newspaper under the title: *Forerunner of Spring*—"Yesterday the first skylark of the year was shot, and brought to the Kings palace." Man had killed the innocent little bird on whose wings Spring had flown to the North, and whose little songster's heart was beating with Nature's jubilant joy! And in the palace they had eaten the gray-coated little messenger of summer! That day the boy swore his Hannibal oath against shooting. And when he fell asleep that night he dreamt about a republican rebellion.

Do not believe that this is nothing but theoretical nonsense—that I am discussing matters of which I know nothing. For there was a time when I felt the fascination of the gun myself; there was a time when I too was a great shot. The man who is now sitting here and scribbling about his love for animals, shoots no more; but it is with an indulgent smile on his lips that he looks back upon the whimsical sportsman of bygone days.

Yes, I have been a sportsman—a great sportsman. I have often made long journeys to join shooting parties, and more than once there was no one in the whole company who fired off as many cartridges as I did. All my best friends were amongst sportsmen, and it was seldom indeed I failed to be present on the opening day of the season. We had lots of good sport about my place, but the best was blackcock-shooting. Do you know anything about blackcock-shooting? A very fine sport. How many pleasant recollections have I not from those happy sporting days! how many joyful rambles through the silent forests! how many peaceful hours passed away in half-waking dreams, with the head leaning against a mossy hillock and soft murmuring pines all around! And how happy, too, was my poor old Tom during these never-to-be-forgotten days of sport! How glad was he to scamper about on the soft moss instead of the stones of the streets! how contentedly he lay down to harmonious contemplations by my side—so near that I could now and then caress his beautiful head and catch a friendly glance from his half-open eyes. He knew I was always in splendid temper on those shooting days, and that was all he required to be perfectly happy himself. But if I begin to speak about my dear old dog we shall never arrive at the blackcock, and it is about them I want to speak to-day.

The gamekeeper had long known the whereabouts of the birds, and carefully exploring the woods he had often enough heard the call of the hen; the blackcock chicks had, so to speak, grown up under his eyes, and he had tried in all sorts of ways to take care of them, the good gamekeeper! And now since they had grown up, the important thing had been to keep them undisturbed lest they should be dispersed. We sportsmen came down the day before the opening day, and well do I remember those pleasant evenings, with a stroll in the forest to clear the lungs from the dust of the town, and then supper in the gamekeeper's cottage in excellent company, flavoured with stories of first-rate shots and marvellous adventures. At first I used to be rather shy, and would silently sit and listen to the others' wonderful tales, but I soon got to learn the trick, and having once mastered the technical terms, I had shot every kind of game at every conceivable range. After dinner, when we got hold of our pipes, I had killed swallows with bullets at tremendous distances, and my friends began to consult me about guns and cartridges and all the other paraphernalia, and were most anxious to have my advice about the arrangements for the next day. Tom lay beside us in the grass and stared with solemn dignity at the company, winking knowingly at me with one eye when no one else was looking, whilst I was telling them about his pedigree and some of his most astounding achievements. When we had delivered ourselves of all our stories, and every one's power of invention had come to an end, we began to yawn, and soon dispersed to our sleeping-quarters to gain strength for next day's hard work.

I remember so well my first blackcock. I had happened to come upon the birds during a short walk with the gamekeeper in the afternoon, and I had heard the mother's anxious call, and had seen some clumsy blackcock children following after her into the forest. I was so excited that I could not close my eyes all night, and could think of nothing but blackcock. Outside, the enchanting summer night allured me to its darkening fells and mysterious woods, and it was as though I could see before my eyes the condemned blackcock where they sat and slept their last sleep. Everything was still in the cottage, and, silent as ghosts, Tom and I glided out armed to the teeth. Yes, I could see the blackcock so distinctly before me, that I had scarcely reached the glen where we had come upon them in the afternoon than I fired off my gun. No blackcock fell. But hardly had the dreadful thunder of the gun died away than the whole forest woke up. Startled small birds fluttered backward and forward deeper into the brushwood. A little squirrel peeped cautiously between two branches, dropped in his fright the fir-cone he was crunching, and then jumped hastily away. The nasty smoke spread with the wind farther in the wood, and pinched the nose of a hare who sat half-asleep under a bush. "I smell human blood," said the hare to himself, like the giant to Tom Thumb, and off he went in a tremendous hurry to find a safer refuge for the day's rest. Tom and I watched him with interest as he stopped short in catching sight of us, stamped with his paws, and then scampered off. The hare has the reputation of being rather ugly; we noticed, on the contrary, that he was quite graceful in his elegant leap over a fallen fir-tree, and I was sorry he did not give us a little longer time in which to look at him. It is not every day one gets a hare; and very satisfied with the beginning of our day, we went on farther into the forest, keeping a sharp look-out for the blackcock. We soon left the forest track and wandered along over the moss, soft as velvet, without the slightest idea where we were going. So we came upon a little brook which cheerfully murmured in our ears as he hurried along, would we not like to accompany him down to the lake? and that we did, to make sure that he did not go astray in the gloom between hillocks and stones. We could not see him, but we heard him singing to himself the whole time. Now and then he stopped short at a jutting rock or fallen tree and waited for us, and then he rushed down the vale quicker than ever to make up for lost time. Yes, it was easy enough for him, who had nothing to carry but some flowers and dry leaves, to rush off with such a speed; he should have had that confounded gun to drag with him, he would then have seen how easy a matter it was! And thus it happened that he ran away from us. We did not know what to do next, so we fired off a shot again. No blackcock fell. But we had scarcely time to load the gun again before we came upon the whole covey. Fancy if I had not had time to load! But they got it all right. There was a tremendous whirring up in the tree-tops, and on heavy wings they dispersed in different directions. We thought the blackcock was a very fine bird, who looks exceedingly well in a forest.

Hallo! There he came again, our friend the brook, dancing toward us happier than ever, and I bent down to kiss his night-cool face just as he glided past me. Ah! now there was no longer any danger that he should lose his way, for already the night had fled away on swift dwarf-feet to hide itself deeper in the forest under the thick firs. Around us birches and aspens put on their green coats, and amongst the moss and fern at our feet small flowers stretched their pretty heads out of the gloom and looked at us as we passed. And deep below in the misty valley a lake opened its eyelid.

So we got sick of blackcock-shooting and we sat down on a mossy stone to read a chapter of Nature's bible whilst the sun rose above the fir-tops and the sky brightened over our heads.

The disturber of the peace sat there quite quiet, silently wondering to himself how it could be possible that men exist who have the heart to bring sorrow and death into a friendly forest. And the small birds also began to wonder, wonder whether that dreadful thunder which awoke them was only a bad dream; the whole forest was so silent again, and perchance it might not be so dangerous to try a little song! And so they took courage one after another and began each to sing their tune. Some were perfect artists and sang long arias with trills and variations; some sang folk-songs; some knew nothing but a little refrain, and that they did not in the least mind repeating over and over again; and some only knew how to hum a single little note, but they were just as merry for all that. And now and again one could hear among all the soprani a rich melodious alto who sang an old ballad—listen! that is the greatest artist in the whole forest; that is the blackbird!

So I thanked my little wild friends for their song; they knew well how happy I felt with them. But I was obliged to turn home again. I told them that I was a sportsman and that I had to be at the rendezvous with my party at seven sharp. I told them to be prudent, to listen carefully for the sound of our voices and to fly on quick wings as soon as we approached—they must be aware that men are so unmusical that they do not know how to appreciate a soulful artist; that they are so unkind, one can never know what may happen. And the merry squirrels, the red-skinned little acrobats of the woods, I told them also to be on the look-out, to take care not to crunch their fir-cones too loudly and not to peep too much from behind their tree—they must know that men are so cold in their hearts that to keep warm they wrap themselves in furs made from their small red coats. I had also prepared a speech for the blackcock, but, as I never caught sight of them again, I could not deliver it. But I had the impression that they had grasped the situation thoroughly, and that was all I wanted of them.

I was punctual at the rendezvous, and the party set off in excellent spirits. We roamed about the whole day, strode miles and miles with our huge game-bags dangling behind our backs, sank knee-deep into morasses and bogs, climbed over hundreds of hedges and tore our faces with the branches of the tangled brushwood. We were all to meet in the evening at the shooting-box, where supper (with roast blackcock) was to be served, and where also, idyllic enough, ladies were to come to give the sportsmen welcome, and to share the spoil.

As one sportsman after the other, hungry and disappointed, reached the meeting-place, dragging his gun after him, those who were already there looked eagerly at his bag. I was one of the last, and I saw at once that the situation was gloomy. I was also in a bad temper, having just discovered that I had unfortunately left my gun behind somewhere, and I could not remember in the least where it might be. I was very disagreeably surprised to see one of the party with a cry of triumph seize hold of my bag. The bag looked really as if it were filled, but the fact was I was absolutely unprepared for such importunate examination. I protested and said it contained nothing but small birds and squirrels, but he took the bag from me and the whole party watched with avaricious eyes when he thrust in his hand and fumbled in the bag. After he had pulled out my whole little shooting-library, Heine and Alfred de Musset and my old friend Leopardi, all the sportsmen looked at each other with amazement. And I quite lost my head. They became absolutely furious when, with my unfortunate absent-mindedness, I happened to let out that I had made a little private excursion before sunrise and by chance had come across some blackcock. "*But had you not time to fire at them?*" they cried, shaking me by the arms and pulling at my coat. "*Yes, of course, I had time to fire, but the blackcock had also time to get away.*" "*Did you not aim at the thick of the covey?*" they yelled with bloodshot eyes and contorted faces. "*No, I think that I aimed at a little cloud, and, for the matter of that, I think I hit it, for a moment later I saw that the sky was beautifully blue.*" My remark about the cloud must have been to the point, for it made them absolutely dumbfounded; they only shook their heads in silence and stared at me while I put my books in the bag again. I had not time to stay longer, having to go and look at the effects of the sunset deeper in the wood, and I politely begged them to excuse me for breaking up the party.

I had not gone many steps before there broke out a frightful dispute amongst them as to who was guilty of having brought me amongst them, and, as far as I could make out, they called me "that idiot."

I was never invited to that place any more. For the matter of that, it was an observation I often made—I was never invited more than once to any place. To my astonishment I saw myself cut out from one house-party after another, and there sprang up a rumour that I brought bad luck with me. Isn't it odd, this often-observed tendency to superstition amongst sportsmen?

I have really no time to linger any longer over my new game-laws, for I have so many other reforms concerning the animals at hand. Only think how much there is to be done for domestic animals also! The division of labour forms here a most important chapter. The domestic animals will only have to work a certain number of hours a day, in proportion to their strength, and not, as now, work themselves to death. And so when age comes upon them men will have to try to give back to the tired animals a small part of all that these humble fellow-workmen have given to them as long as they were able. Surely the domestic animals belong to the family; and just as the old labourer is allowed to end his days in peace in his little cottage, so shall the old horse, when his eyes begin to grow dim and his legs to get stiff, be allowed to rest in his stall; and now and then one should go and pet the old servant with grateful hands, and give him his bit of bread as before. The old worn-out ox, surely he too might be allowed at last to glean a little dry hay from the fields which he in his strong days has so many times ploughed for the seed, which year after year filled the farmer's barn with golden sheaves and sweet clover. And the kind, sympathetic little donkeys, whose whole life is a series of self-renunciation, and whose melancholy is an unheard protest against the degradation into which they have fallen—surely I shall not forget you in my reforms, my poor Italian friends! And keep up your courage, resigned little donkeys! your cause is a good one, the tyranny of barbarians shall come to an end one day, and the oppressed animals shall be given back their right to enjoy life, even they! And the day will come when you are to be reinstated in the high social position which your misunderstood intelligence and your subtle humour entitle you to hold, and when you shall throw back in the faces of your oppressors the epithet which short-sighted men now apply to you!

The sanitary condition of animals is to be improved a great deal. Hospitals and asylums for sick and aged animals are to be founded. Up till now I know personally of only two almshouses, that in London for "lost and starving dogs"—where they are not so badly cared for—and that in Florence for aged and infirm cats—it includes a *crèche* for lost and orphan kittens (it has been founded by an English lady, I believe).

The jurisdiction is to be entirely changed. Flogging is only to be allowed in certain exceptional cases, and only after serious remonstrances and repeated warnings. There is nothing in the whole of creation so stubborn as a schoolboy when he tries his best; well, now, when one is no longer allowed to flog him, why may one then be allowed to beat the animal whose duller perception ought so much the more to protect him from the birch-rod?

Capital execution—I recognise its necessity—is to be changed from arbitrary barbarity to an institution watched over by mildness and tenderness for the condemned animal. The animal-executioners should form a corporation apart, kept under the severest supervision. The profession is a repulsive but a necessary one, and the individuals who enlist themselves on its roll deserve high wages.

It was never meant that man should be an autocratic tyrant in the great society which peoples the world, but a constitutional monarch. I had dreamt of a republic, but I admit that our earth is not yet ripe for this form of government. Yes, man is the ruler of the earth; always victorious, he carries his blood-stained banner round the world, and his kingdom has no longer any limit. But man is an upstart—I, at any rate, cannot believe all his talk about his high birth. He will try to take us in by saying that he is a foundling who was mysteriously put into the nursery of creation, and that he is of far nobler origin than anybody else on the whole earth. It is true there is something peculiar about him, and that he is domineering and arrogant: that he showed early enough. Even when a baby, and lying at Nature's mother-breast, he pushed away the other children of the earth, and drank the strength of life in deep draughts. Hardly could he crawl before he scratched his kind nurse in the face and beat his weaker foster-brothers. So he grew up to be a true bully, a brutish Protanthropos, breaking down each obstacle, subduing with the right of the stronger all opposition. And the law of selection enlarged his facial angle, and culture put arms in his hands. How could the sickle-like claws of *Ursus spelæus* (cave-bear) prevail against his trident studded with thorns or twig-spikes or set with razor-edged shells? What could the six-inch long canines of Machærodus do against his sharpened flint? And so they disappeared, one after the other, these vanquished giants, into the gloom of past ages. But the power of man expanded more and more, and higher and higher flew his thoughts. Now the earth lies at his feet, and he prepares to assault heaven! And he has been so spoiled by all his success, so refined by all civilisation, that he turns up his aristocratic nose whenever one reminds him of his childhood. And his humble old ancestors, among whom his cradle stood, and all his poor relations who, homeless, rove about the earth, these he will not own at all, and he is so hard to them. But man is no longer young—no one knows exactly how many hundred thousand years he carries on his back; but I think it is time for him to reflect a little upon all the evil he has done in his days, and try to grow a little kinder in his old age. The day will come when the last man will lie down to die, and when a new-crowned king of creation will mount the throne—*le roi est mort, vive le roi!* So falls the twilight of ages round the sarcophagus where the dead monarch sleeps in the Pantheon of Palæontology. The dust covers the inscription which records all the honorary titles of the dead, and the standards which witnessed his victories moulder away. Up there in the new planet sits a professor, and lectures about the remains from prehistoric times, and he hands round to his audience a fragile cranium, which is carefully examined by wondering students. It is our cranium, with that upright facial angle and that large brain-pan which was our pride! And the professor makes a casual remark about *Homo Sapiens*, and he points out the fang which is still to be seen in the jaw.

We learn from the long story of the development of our race that the hunter-stage was the lowest of all human conditions, the most purely animal. The pursuing and killing of animals for mere pleasure is a humiliating reminiscence from this time of savagery. Man's right over the animal is limited to his right of defence, and his right of existence. The former can only very seldom be evoked in our country; the latter cannot be evoked by our class.

A man of culture recognises his obligations towards animals as a compensation for the servitude he imposes on them. The pursuing and killing of animals for mere pleasure is incompatible with the fulfilment of these obligations. Sympathy extending beyond the limit of humanity, *i.e.* kindness to animals, is one of the latest moral qualities acquired by mankind. This sympathy is absolutely lacking in the lowest human races, and the degree of this sympathy possessed by an individual marks the distance which separates him from his primitive state of savagery.

An individual who enjoys the pursuing and killing of animals is thus to be considered as a transitional type between a savage and a man of culture. He forms the missing link in the evolution of the mind from brutishness to humanity.

TO ——

"The firmest friend, The first to welcome, foremost to defend." BYRON.

We have camped together for the whole of ten years. We have stuck to each other in both joy and sorrow; honestly we have shared good and evil.

When I am happy he is also happy; he does not for a moment consider if he has any personal reason to cheer up; he doesn't ask for any explanations; he only thinks of partaking in my pleasure—only a glance, a nod, or a single friendly word is enough for him, and his whole honest face lights up with my joy. And when I am depressed and miserable, he then sits so sorrowfully by my side. He does not try to console me, for he knows how little words of pity avail; he says nothing, for he knows that silence is a comfort when one is sad. He only looks steadfastly at me, and maybe puts his big head on my knee. He knows that he cannot fathom what it is that worries me; that his poor, dark brain cannot follow me in all I am thinking about; but his faithful heart anyhow wants to claim his share of my burden.

Others think I am quick-tempered and angry, and pay me back in the same way; his patient indulgence knows how to forgive everything; his friendship stands the trial against all injustice. Am I nervous and hard on him when I leave him, he rewards evil with good and comes just as friendly and caressingly to meet me when I come back. Others sit in judgment over my many faults, and have only words of blame for whatever I take in hand; he tries with loving eagerness to find out the least ugly side of everything; he refuses to believe me capable of anything wrong. When I defend a cause, I am too often considered to be in the wrong; but he thinks always as I do. In the moment of adversity no friends are to be found; he is always at my side ready to defend me against any peril, happy, if required, to give his life for mine.

He never complains; he is always satisfied, however uncomfortable he is, if only he may be allowed to be with me. He can sit for hours out in the street waiting patiently, in cold and rain, whilst I am visiting some of my acquaintances where he is not received. Is there no room in the carriage when I drive, he runs just as cheerfully behind me; he is even delighted when I am driving; he is proud of me; he thinks it looks grand. Do I go out in my boat, without hesitation he jumps in the water after me; he swims as long as he has any breath left, and when his strength begins to give out, with a last effort he raises himself out of the water to look after the boat, but to return to the shore he never dreams of. When I travel by train, he sits, without complaining, cramped up in his little compartment for however long it may be, without a scrap of comfort, with the sharp wind blowing straight through, sore in all his bones with the continual shaking, softened by no springs, black in his face as a sweep from the smoke of the engine. And anyhow, whenever the train stops, he shouts out cheerfully that he is there, and all well on board. Have I time to run forward and look at him, he peeps out patiently and contentedly through his little barred window, and presses his dry nose against my hand—never a hint that he is aware how uncomfortable he is, compared to me in my luxurious wagon-lit; never the slightest complaint against the railway company who has done so surprisingly little for travellers of his class.

But if he, out of delicacy for me, has never wanted to make any complaint, I do not see why I should be kept back from doing so by any such consideration. And I may as well tell you that I am thinking of getting up a petition to protest against *the unfair distribution of comfort for railway travellers*. I have been inquiring about it for the many years I have knocked about on the railways of all nations, and I am pretty sure that I may count upon a great number of signatures from travellers concerned. Man, who always takes the best of everything, and thinks of nobody but himself, has also succeeded in securing all sorts of advantages from the railway companies—advantages which exclusively benefit him, but which are a crying injustice towards other travellers, who have also paid for their tickets, and consequently have a right, even they, to claim the fulfilment of the obligations which the railway company has accepted towards them. If I am waked up in the night in my comfortable berth by the heating apparatus having gone wrong, and find the compartment cold, I have only to complain to the conductor; but I have innumerable times heard loud complaints from the dog-compartments about the ice-cold night-wind blowing straight through them, and I have never noticed any one pay the slightest attention to this. If my neighbour lights a cigar, and having blown a cloud of smoke in my face, asks me if I object to his smoking, although it is not a smoking compartment, I have only to answer "Yes," to get rid of the smoke; but who has ever asked the dogs if they object to the thick fumes of coal which the engine puffs in their faces the whole time, where the poor fellows sit in the front van?

All trains stop at certain places for refreshment, and we have only to run into the buffet to eat our fill; but is there any one who knows how difficult it is to get a little food and a drink of water for a travelling dog? The minutes are counted, and you are served in turn as you come to the buffet, you believe. No, not in the very least, the dogs are always skipped over, even if they have their money lying ready before them on the table; and as often as not, when their turn comes the bell rings, and the train is off. When I was in the first stage of my human knowledge—the Idealistic—I always asked for some food for my dog; that was no good, no waiter was kind enough to listen to that. Later, when in the second stage—that of Vanishing Illusions—I asked at once for a beefsteak for my dog; that was not much better, the chances of getting anything are very small. In the third stage—that of Hopeless Pessimism—I immediately ask for dinner for two, and turn two chairs at the *table d'hôte*; Tappio disappears instantly under the table, and I hand down to him his portion as it is placed before his chair. I have acquired such a practice in this that nobody notices where the food goes, and silent as a ghost, Tappio swallows down both cutlets and pastry in one gulp—the only thing which has made him lose countenance has been the, in Italy, not uncommon practice of serving ice-cream, of the inconvenience of which, at railway dinners, I agree with him. I remember how once in Macon—the Paris-Turin night-train used to stop there for supper—we had as neighbours a peaceful family of bourgeois, the members of which, one after the other, dropped their knives and forks as the dinner proceeded, and stared at me and my rapidly vanishing double portions with increasing amazement. At last a little old lady, who was of the party, exclaimed, quite aloud, "*Voilà un homme que je ne voudrais pas inviter à dîner, il serait capable de manger les assiettes aussi!*"

Yes, we have seen a good deal of the world; we have met many people on our way; our experience of life is large enough. There was a time when we were ambitious we also, very ambitious. We dreamt of prize medals and certificates for both of us, of Persian carpets under our feet, and of roasted ortolans flying straight into our mouths. That time is past, one of us is already gray, but no roasted ortolans have flown into our mouths, nor any Persian carpets spread themselves under our feet. And when the floor feels too cold, I lay down my cloak for my comrade to lie upon. And we begin to realise what man is worth. We used to be idealists because we believed that others were idealists. We were gentle and harmless as lambs because we believed that others were so. We were philanthropists. But we have discovered that we were mistaken. Men are not at all kind to each other. They talk so much about friendship, but there are only very few of them who are capable of realising the true signification of this word.

But, to be sure, they laugh if one gives to a dog's faithful devotion the name of friendship, if with thankful recognition one strives to repay as far as lies in one's power the humble comrade whom they call but a soulless animal, whose fine, sensitive thought they call instinct, and for whose honest, noble soul they deny all right to live any longer than his faithful dog-heart beats.

If this be not virtue, this all-sacrificing, all-self-denying, all-injustice-forgetting love,—well, then, I don't know what virtue means; and should his only reward for a whole life's faithful devotion consist in being shot in his old age and buried under a tree in the park at home, then all I say is, that I do not believe that we either will get beyond the grave where our remains will one day be laid.

MONSIEUR ALFREDO

I do not in the least know how I happened to come upon the modest little café, nor do I know how it came to pass that during the whole of that year I frequented no other.

I wonder whether it was not on account of Monsieur Alfredo that I became an habitué there.

He evidently had his luncheon later than I, as I had already had time to smoke a couple of cigarettes before he made his appearance at the Café de l'Empereur, upright and trim in his tightly-buttoned frock-coat, a roll of manuscript under his arm, and his gray hair in neat curls surrounding his wrinkled, childlike face. The waiter brought him his little cup of coffee and placed the chess-board between us. Monsieur Alfredo, with old-fashioned courtesy, inquired after my health, and I on my side received satisfactory assurances as to his well-being. I busied myself in placing the chess-men, and whilst I groped under the table to find that pawn which somehow or other had always fallen to the ground, Monsieur Alfredo rapidly produced his lump of sugar out of his pocket and put it into his cup.

We always played two games. I am singularly unlucky in games, and the old man, who loved chess, beamed all over every time he checkmated me. He played very slowly, but with amazing boldness, and even after having played with him every day for months together, I was still incapable of forming an opinion as to which of us played the worse. What puzzled me most of all was the fact that Monsieur Alfredo seldom or never played anything but kings and queens; occasionally, with reluctance, he would put the knights, castles, and bishops into requisition, but as to the pawns, he appeared to ignore them altogether. I had never before seen anybody play in this way, and often enough had I to look very sharp to make sure of losing.

The conversation turned on literature, and above all, the theatre. Monsieur Alfredo was extremely exacting as to dramatic art, and approved of no other form than the tragic. He was exceedingly difficult as to authors. I was just then full of Victor Hugo, but Monsieur Alfredo considered him much too sentimental. Racine and Corneille he thought better of, although he gave me to understand he considered them lacking in power. He despised comedy and refused point-blank to admit Scribe, Augier, Labiche, or Dumas as celebrities. One only needed to mention the name of Offenbach or Lecocq to make the otherwise peaceful Monsieur Alfredo fall into a complete rage; he then burst forth into Italian, which he never spoke unless greatly excited; he denounced them as *Birbanti*, and *Avvelenatori*,[20]—they had with their music spread the poison which had killed the good taste of a whole generation, and they were, to a great extent, responsible for the downfall of tragedy in our days.

He seemed well informed in everything concerning the Paris theatres, and was evidently a frequent playgoer himself; I had once or twice hinted that we should go to the theatre together some evening, but had observed that Monsieur Alfredo never seemed willing to understand me.

As soon as we had finished our second game, Monsieur Alfredo produced four sous wrapped up in paper, called the waiter and asked what he had to pay, and laid his four sous on the table. The Café de l'Empereur was not a very expensive place, as you may perceive; on the Boulevard St. Michel they charged you eight sous for a cup of coffee, here you only had to pay four if you took it without milk or sugar—Monsieur Alfredo had long ago confided to me his experience that sugar took away half the fragrance of coffee. I, who was not so particular, had both sugar and milk with my coffee, and cognac besides, but never once had I succeeded in getting Monsieur Alfredo to accept a glass from me. I had tried to tempt him with everything the Café de l'Empereur could offer, but the old gentleman had always declined courteously but firmly.

I knew that Monsieur Alfredo was an author, and that it was the manuscript of a five-act tragedy he carried under his arm. I have always admired authors and artists, and I tried my best to make him understand how flattered I felt by his society. I had long ago told him everything about myself and my affairs, but Monsieur Alfredo showed for a long while a singular reticence in all that concerned himself. Sometimes, on leaving the café together, I had tried to accompany him for a while, but, once in the streets, he always wished me good-bye, and I could easily see that I was not wanted. I had also expressed a wish to be allowed to call upon him, but had been given to understand that his time was very limited just then, and feeling sure that the tragedy was the cause of it all, I took good care not to disturb him.

He never came to the café in the evening, so I then lounged there alone smoking. Every now and then I dined with some of my fellow-students down on the boulevards, but as true inhabitants of the Quartier Latin, it was only seldom that we crossed the Seine. One evening, however, some one at the dinner-table proposed that we should all drive down to the Variétés to see Offenbach's *Les Brigands*, and somehow or another they carried me off with them.

I believe the whole pit was full of students. We were in tremendous spirits, and applauded quite as vigorously as the *claque* which occupied the row behind us. It seemed to me as though I were playing my old friend from the Café de l'Empereur false, and I felt how he would despise me had he seen me, and I made up my mind not to tell him anything about it. But I could not help it, I roared with laughter the whole time. The last words of a song were hardly over before the *claque* broke out with a deafening applause, and we and the whole pit followed their lead with right good will. And so when we collapsed and could move our arms no longer, the *claque* had recuperated its strength, and the brilliant farce was hailed once more with thundering applause by the joyless spectators behind us, where a whole chorus of poor devils shouted "bravo, bravo!" for next day's bread.

Suddenly I was startled by a "bravo, bravo!" which came a little after the rest. I turned rapidly round, and ran my eye over the *claque*, and then to the astonishment of my comrades, I took my hat and slunk out of the theatre.

The joyous music rang in my ears the whole way home, but I felt that tears were not far from my eyes that night.

No, I never told Monsieur Alfredo that I had been to see *Les Brigands*. I never alluded again in our conversations to Offenbach and Lecocq, and never more did I try to accompany the old gentleman to the theatre.

Next day, after we had finished our game of chess, I followed him home at some little distance. I went to his house that same evening, and whilst I stood there contemplating the card on Monsieur Alfredo's door, the concierge made her appearance, and informed me that he never spent the evenings at home. "Was I perhaps a pupil?" I answered in the affirmative. I asked her if he had many pupils just then, and she answered I was the first she had ever seen.

It was towards the end of autumn that I communicated to Monsieur Alfredo my irrevocable decision to throw medicine to the winds and to devote myself to the stage, and to my great satisfaction he consented to become my instructor in deportment and declamation. The lessons were given at my rooms in the Hôtel de l'Avenir. The old fellow's method was a peculiar one, and his theories on acting as bold as those he held on chess. I listened with the utmost attention to all he said, and tried as well as I could to learn the fundamental rules of deportment he saw fit to teach me. After a while he acceded to my request to be allowed to try myself in a rôle, and fully aware of my preference for tragedy, it was decided that, under the immediate superintendence of the author himself, I should get up one of the characters in Monsieur Alfredo's last work, *Le Poignard*, a tragedy in five acts. Monsieur Alfredo himself was the king and I was the marquis. I admit that my début was not a happy one. I saw that the author was far from satisfied with me, and I realised myself that my marquis was a dead failure. My next début was in the rôle of the English lord in the five-act tragedy, *La Vengeance*, but neither there were there any illusions possible as to my success. I then tried my luck as the count in *Le Secret du Tombeau*, but with a very doubtful result. I then sank down to a viscount, and made superhuman efforts to keep up to the mark, but notwithstanding the indulgent way in which Monsieur Alfredo pointed out my shortcomings, I could not conceal from myself the fact that I was not fit to be a viscount either.

I began to have serious doubts as to my theatrical vocation, but Monsieur Alfredo thought that the reason of my failure might be traced to my unfamiliarity with the highest society, and my difficulty in adapting myself to the sensations and thoughts of these high personages. And he was right—it was anything but easy. All his heroes and heroines were very sorry for themselves, not to say desperate, although as a rule it was impossible for me to understand the reason of their being so. Love and hatred glowed in every one's eyes. True that as a rule everything went wrong for the lovers, but even if they got each other at last, they did not seem to be a bit the more cheerful for that. I remember, for instance, the third act of *Le Poignard*, where I (the marquis), after having waded through blood, succeed in winning the lady of my heart, who on her side has gone through fire and water to be mine. The Archbishop marries us by moonlight, and we, who had not seen each other for ten years, are left alone for a while in a bower of roses. We had nothing on earth to be afraid of; no one was likely to disturb us, as I had previously run my sword through every grown-up person in the play, and I thought that I ought to be a little kind to the marchioness. But Monsieur Alfredo never found my voice tragic enough during the few brief moments of happiness he granted us. (We perished shortly afterwards in an earthquake.)

For the matter of that, those who escaped a violent death were not much better off—they were carried off in any case in the flower of their youth by sudden inexplicable ailments, which no amount of care could contend against. At first I tried to save some of the victims, but Monsieur Alfredo always looked very astonished when I suggested that some one might be allowed to recover; and knowing his theory that it was sentimentality that spoiled Victor Hugo as a dramatist, I ceased more and more to interfere in the matter.

After a few more abortive attempts to pose as a nobleman, I submitted to Monsieur Alfredo my opinion that I might do better in a more humble position. But here we were met by an unforeseen obstacle—Monsieur Alfredo did not descend below viscounts. If by the exigencies of the plot a lonely representative of the lower orders had to appear on the scene, he had no sooner got a word out of his mouth before the author would fling a purse at his head, and send him back into the wings with an imperial wave of his shiny coat sleeve. Well, away with all false pride! It was in these rôles I at last hit upon my true genre; it was here I scored my only triumphs. Imperceptibly to the old man, I disappeared more and more from the répertoire, would now and then cross the stage and with a deep obeisance deliver a manuscript letter from some crowned head, or would occasionally come to carry off a corpse—that was all.

So the autumn passed on, we had gone through one tragedy after another, and still Monsieur Alfredo constantly turned up with a new manuscript under his arm. I began to be afraid that the old man would wear himself out with this fathomless authorship, and I tried in every possible way to make him rest a little. This was, however, quite impossible. He now came every single day to Hôtel de l'Avenir to his only pupil and literary confidant. His guileless, childish face seemed to grow more and more gentle, and more and more was I drawn towards the poor old enthusiast with a sort of tender sympathy.

And unquenchable and ever more unquenchable became his literary bloodthirstiness. By Christmas-time his new tragedy was ready, and Monsieur Alfredo himself looked upon it as his best work. The scene was laid in Sicily at the foot of Mount Etna in the midst of burning lava-streams. Not a soul survived the fifth act. I begged for the life of a Newfoundland dog, who, with a dead heir in his mouth, had swum over from the mainland, but Monsieur Alfredo was inexorable. The dog threw himself into the crater of Etna in the last scene.

But while the lava of Mount Etna was heating Monsieur Alfredo's world of dreams, the winter snow was falling over Paris. All of us had long since taken to our winter coats, but my poor professor was still wandering about in his same old frock-coat, so shiny with constant brushing, so thread-bare with the wear and tear of years. The nights became so cold, and sadly did I follow in my thoughts the poor old man tramping home every night across the streets of Paris after the theatre was over. Many times was I very near broaching the delicate subject, but was always deterred by the sensitive pride with which he sought to disguise his poverty. Yet had I never seen him in such excellent spirits as he was just then, he placed greater expectations than ever on his new tragedy. Like all his previous plays it was written for the Théâtre Français. The systematic ill-will with which Mons. Perrin[21] had refused to accept any work of his had certainly made him turn his thoughts to the Odéon Theatre; but with due consideration to the colossal proportions of his new drama, Monsieur Alfredo did not quite see how to avoid offering it to the very first theatre in Paris.

Maybe it seems to you that I ought to have pointed out to Monsieur Alfredo the dangerous flights of his imagination, that I ought to have tried to make him realise that his theatre was erected on quite another planet than ours. I did nothing of the sort, and you would not have done so either had you known him as I did, had you witnessed the anxiety with which his kind eyes sought for my approval, how his sad old child-face brightened up when he recited some passage which he expected would especially dumbfound me—

which alas! it seldom failed to do. But I had arrived so far that I was quite incapable of spoiling his pleasure by a single word of criticism. Silently I listened to tragedy after tragedy, and there was no need to simulate being serious, for all my laughter over his wild creations was silenced by the tragedy of reality, all my criticism was disarmed by his utter helplessness—he did not even possess an overcoat! The only audience the poor old man ever had was me, why then shouldn't I bestow upon him a little approval, he whom life had so unmercifully hissed?

One afternoon he did not turn up at the Café de l'Empereur, and in vain I waited for him before the chess-board the next day. I waited still another day, but then, driven by uneasy forebodings, I went to look him up towards evening. The concierge had not seen him go out, and there was no answer to my knock at his door. I stood there for a moment or two looking at the faded old visiting-card nailed on his door—

Mr. ALFREDO

Auteur Dramatique

Professeur de Déclamation, de Maintien

et de Mise en Scène.

And then I quietly opened the door and went in.

The old man lay on his bed delirious, not recognising the unbidden guest who stood there, sadly looking round the empty garret cold as the streets without, for there was no fireplace.

It was sunny and bright next day, and it was easy to remove him to the hospital close by—I was on the staff there for the matter of that. He had pneumonia. They were all very kind to the old gentleman, both the doctors and the students, and dear Soeur Philomène managed matters so successfully that she got a private room for him. He continued delirious the whole of that day and night, but towards morning he became conscious and recognised me. He then insisted on returning at once to his own quarters, but quieted down considerably on being told he was in a private room, and that he was quite independent of all the other patients. After some hesitation he inquired what he would have to pay, and I answered him I did not think the hospital could charge him anything, as the *Société des Auteurs Dramatiques* was entitled to a free bed, and I doubted whether it would be the right thing to refuse to avail himself of this privilege, as of course every one knew who he was. Soeur Philomène, who stood behind his pillow, shook her finger reprovingly at my little white lie, but I could well see by the expression of her eyes that she forgave me. I had touched the poor old author's most sensitive chord; with keenest interest he made me repeat over and over again what I had said about the *Société des Auteurs Dramatiques* and a faint smile of content lit up his faded old face when at last I had succeeded in making him believe me. From that moment he seemed quite pleased and satisfied with everything, and he did not realise himself how rapidly he was sinking. According to his wish, a little table with writing materials had been placed beside his bed, but he had not yet tried to write anything.

The night had been worse than usual, and during the morning round I noticed that Soeur Philomène had hung a little crucifix at the head of his bed. He lay there quite silent the whole day, once only when he was given his broth he asked for the name of the most rapid poison, and Soeur Philomène thought it was prussic acid.

Towards evening he became more feverish, and his eyes began to be restless. He begged me to sit down beside him, and after swearing me over to secrecy he unveiled to me the plot of his new tragedy where the rival gives prussic acid to the bride and bridegroom during the wedding ceremony. He spoke rapidly and cheerfully, and with a triumphant glance he asked me whether I thought the Théâtre Français would dare to reject him this time, and I answered that I did not believe it would dare to do so. The work was to proceed with great speed, the first act was to be ready next morning, and in a week's time at the very latest he intended to send in the manuscript for perusal.

He became more and more delirious, and he did not pay any more attention to my answers. His eye still rested on mine, but his horizon widened more and more, for the barriers of this world began to fall away. His speech became more and more rapid, and I could no longer follow his staggering thought. But his face still expressed what his failing perception could no longer form into words, and with deep emotion I witnessed death bestow on him the joy that life had denied him.

He seemed to listen. There flew a light over his pale features, his eye sparkled, and with head erect the old man sat up in bed. He shook away his gray curls, and a shimmer of triumph fell over his brow. With his hand on his heart the dying author made a low bow, for in the silence of the falling night he heard the echo of his life's fondest dream; he heard the Théâtre Français jubilant with applause!

And slowly the curtain sank upon the old author's last tragedy.

MONT BLANC

KING OF THE MOUNTAINS

Mont Blanc is the monarch of mountains; They crown'd him long ago On a throne of rocks, in a robe of clouds, With a diadem of snow. BYRON.

Note.—The following paper may perhaps be considered rather too whimsical by those unacquainted with a little adventure I had while descending Mont Blanc, an adventure which began in an avalanche and ended happily in a crevasse. The article dances away on the rope of a single metaphor, and dances over precipices. But the sentiment reflected in the word-picture of the title impresses me still so strongly, so much do I still admire the anger of the mighty snow-mountain, that I dare not approach it with the familiarity of a reporter. I see that here and there I have tried to smile—that is because of the pain in my frozen foot. When I make fun of Mont Blanc I am reminded of an antique bas-relief once seen in Rome, representing a little Satyr, who, a look of blank astonishment on his face, measures the toe of a sleeping Polyphemus.

The ascent of Mont Blanc is easy.

No one attempts the *Weisshorn*, *Dent Blanche*, or the *Matterhorn* unless his eye be calm and his foot sure, but we all know that Tartarin of Tarascon went up Mont Blanc—although he never arrived at the top.

They are indomitable revolutionists, these other mountain giants, freedom's untamed heroes who refuse to be subjugated save by the sun alone, haughty lords of the Alps who know themselves to be princes of the blood.

But Mont Blanc is the crowned king of the Alps. There was a time when he was sullen and cruel, but he has grown kinder-hearted in his old age, and now, like a venerable patriarch, he sits there, the white-haired Charlemagne, looking out in calm majesty over his three kingdoms.

Good-humouredly he suffers the Lilliputians to crawl up the marble-bright steps that lead into his citadel, and with royal hospitality he allows them to visit his ice-shining castle.

But when the summer day begins to darken into autumn, he goes to sleep in his white state bed under a canopy of clouds. And then he does not like to be disturbed, the old king.

No, he does not like to be disturbed; I knew it well. I had addressed myself to his retainers and had been told that it was too late for an audience, that the king did not receive at this time. I had come from afar, my knapsack on my back, my head full of wonderful stories about the far-famed palace, and longing to see the proud old mountain-king.

Somewhat disconcerted I hung for a while about the castle gates, muttering socialistic sentences to myself. I had taken in radical newspapers all the summer and was not to be treated in that off-hand way. It is the lot of the great to be subjected to the gaze of inquisitive eyes, and I can but be turned away, thought I to myself, and up I went with two followers. Perhaps it was a trifle unceremonious on my part, but I am not used to the court etiquette of conventionality.

Summer accompanied me a little way; at first she climbed the slopes with ease, planting her foot firmly in the clefts, but it was not difficult to see that she, the fair daughter of the valley, did not look forward to the royal visit as ardently as I did. I had got myself up in court-dress to pay my respects to the ice-gray monarch, in sharp-spiked mountain shoes, snow gaiters, and steel-pointed pilgrim staff, but she was in no wise equipped to meet the requirements of such a journey, poor little one! The wind pulled and tugged at her leaf-woven petticoat, and sharp stones cut her green velvet shoes adorned with bows of harebell and forget-me-not. But she did not give in so easily; she bound her poor feet with soft moss; she patched her petticoat with bracken and juniper, and although her fingers were stiff-frozen, neatly and gracefully she managed to weave some tiny heather-bells between.

And thus we reached the summit of a rock, and on the edge thereof sat Cerberus, the fierce sentinel of the castle, barking and howling and shaking his arctic fur till great white tufts flew in the air around. I have never been afraid of bad-tempered dogs and hailed old Boreas by his name and asked him in our own language if he did not recognise me, he, the guardian of my childhood's home. And sure enough he rushed at me full speed! He laid his paws upon my breast with such force that he nearly knocked me backward over the cliff, and licked my face with his icy tongue till I could hardly breathe. But suddenly, in the midst of his friendly demonstrations, he bit my nose, and, what is more, he nearly bit it off—that is what I have always said, one cannot be too careful where strange dogs are concerned! If any one is a lover of dogs I am, but I did not know how to take that, and hurried on as quickly as possible. He evidently thought he belonged to the party, and followed us growling like the brute that he was. But Summer took fright and said she dared not go any farther, and so we took leave of each other. Light-footed and joyous she returned to the green of the alpine meadows, and I, drawing my coat closer round me, went on my way. Some firs also took courage, and, gripping the rugged granite with sinewy arms, they followed us up the rock.

Steeper and steeper became the track, fewer and fewer the green-clad bodyguard which advanced with me. And soon the last of them halted beneath the shelter of a jutting rock. I asked them if they would not come a little farther, but they shook their white heads and bade me farewell. Deeper and deeper penetrated the chill of death into the mountain's veins; slower and slower beat the heart of Nature; higher and higher went my path. And there she stood, the last outpost of Summer, the courageous little child-flower of the mountain heights, beautiful as her name, *Edelweiss*! She stood there quite alone with her feet in the snow; no living soul had she to bear her company, but she was just as neat for all that in her gray little woollen gown edged with frost pearls, and just as frankly for all that did she look up at the sun. She also had her part to play, and it was not for me to do her any harm. I glanced at her a moment and thought how pretty she was, although so simply dressed in her homespun clothes, poor little half-frozen Cinderella amongst her summer-fair sisters of the valley.

I stood now on the frontier of the kingdom of Eternal Winter, and firm of foot I crossed the moat of frozen glacier-waves which surrounded the citadel of the ice-monarch. There reigned a desolate repose over the sleeping palace, and I felt that I was drawing nigh unto a king. I wandered through deserted castle-halls on whose dazzling white carpets no human foot had ever trod, beneath crystal-glittering temple vaults through which the organ thundered like the roar of a subterranean river, between tall colonnades whose cloud-hidden capitals supported the firmament.

So I gained the highest tower of the castle. The winding staircase leading thereunto was gone, but with ice-axe and rope we assaulted the Royal Eagle's nest.

And I stood face to face with the mountain-king. Upon the giant's forehead sat the beaming diadem of the sun, and an unspeakable splendour of purple and gold fell over his royal mantle. No echo from the valleys disturbed his proud repose; mournful in isolated peace he sat on high surveying his mute kingdom. Silent stood the bodyguard about his throne, the tall grenadiers with steel-glinting ice armour upon their granite breasts and cloud-crested helmets upon their snow-white heads. I knew the weather-beaten features of more than one of them full well, and reverently I greeted the giants by name, *Schreckhorn, Wetterhorn, Finsteraarhorn, Monte Rosa, Monte Viso*, and her, the virgin warrior with lowered vizor over her beautiful face immaculate as Diana in her snow-white garb, *Die Jungfrau*! And my eye dwelt long upon the proud combatant yonder, Achilles-like in his god-forged armour purpled with blood, the *Matterhorn*!

But suddenly the king's face darkened and a sombre cloud fell over his forehead. He took off his crown, and his white curls flew in the wind, and without paying the slightest attention to us he put on his night-cap.[22] And we understood that the audience was ended.

But he must be a good sleeper indeed if he be able to rest in such a noise as this, thought we, for around us there arose a fearful tumult. The storm raged over our heads till we thought the roof of the castle would fall in upon us, and Boreas, like a hungry wolf, howled at our heels. Hastily we retraced our steps through the darkening palace; through deserted courtyards where spirit hands swept every trace of path away; through vast state halls, gloomy as chambers of death in their white draperies; through vaults adown which the organ stormed as on the Day of Judgment.

But there was something wrong with these old castle-halls—I began to think they were haunted. There were groans and shrieks; a shrill and scornful laugh rang suddenly through the air, and beside us flew long shadows swathed in white—it was not easy to make out what they were; mountain-wraiths, I suppose.

We then reached a big plain called "*le grand plateau*," but we had hardly got halfway across it before a cannon shot rent the skies. I looked up to see the white smoke dancing down the Mont Maudit and a whole mountain of projectiles bearing down upon us with the speed of an avalanche—*Sapristi!* On we went. Then there came a crash as though the thunder had burst over our heads, the ground gaped under our feet, and I fell into Hades. Everything became silent and the chill of death fell over me.

But the instinct of self-preservation roused me, and half awake I sat up in the coffin and looked around. At the same moment one of my companions also crept out of his shroud, and by the help of the ice-axe we forced open the lid that had already been screwed down over our third companion. And to our astonishment we discovered that we were not dead at all. We sat imprisoned in a subterranean dungeon waiting for trial, but we all agreed that we were in the cell of the condemned. Daylight fell through a narrow rift over our heads, and beside us yawned a great chasm—it was like the Mamertine prison in Rome. We had time to meditate upon a good many things. To complain was useless; to protest against our fate was useless too; all we could do was to hope that the judicial formalities might be conducted as quickly as possible— *der Tod ist nichts, aber das Sterben ist eine schändliche Erfindung!*[23]

Now and then a white wraith peeped through the opening and with mocking laugh threw down great heaps of snow, then swept away over our heads. "Are you still the lords of the earth, you miserable little human microbes?" they howled until the vault shook again. We clenched our teeth and said nothing. At last I got quite angry and shouted back to them that they were nothing but microbes themselves. I glanced at my companions and all three of us made a sort of grimace to show how excellent we thought the joke, but it did not come to much, for the muscles of laughter had been paralysed in our blue faces. But the wraiths seemed taken aback all the same, and, summoning up all my courage, I went on calling out that it was useless to give themselves such airs, that there was something higher than Mont Blanc itself, and I pointed towards a star which just then glanced down at us poor devils through the gray fog bars of the opening. I had hardly got the words out of my mouth before the wraiths vanished one and all, and by the light of the brightening evening we saw that they had been transformed into huge blocks of ice, which, impelled by the avalanche, had stopped short at the very edge of the crevasse—witchcraft, nothing but witchcraft! But it was not witchcraft that got us out that time. It was something else that helped us— that which is higher than Mont Blanc.

RAFFAELLA

The picture was considered one of the very best in the whole Salon, and the young painter's name was on every one's lips. It was always surrounded by a group of admirers, fascinated by its beauty. She lay there on a couch of purple, and around her loveliness there fell as it were a shimmer from life's May-sun. Refined art-critics had settled her age to be at most sixteen. There was still something of the enchanting grace of the child in her slender limbs, and it was as if a veil of innocence protected her.

Who was she, the fair sleeper, the shaping of whose features was so noble, the harmony of whose limbs was so perfect? Was it true, what rumour whispered, that the original of the dazzling picture bore one of the greatest names of France, that a high-born beauty of Faubourg St. Germain had, unknown to the man, allowed the artist to behold the ideal he had sought for but never found? Who was she?

The doctor had stood there for a while listening to the murmur of praise which bore witness to the young painter's triumph, and slowly making his way through the fashionable crowd he approached the exit. He stopped there for a moment or two watching one carriage after another roll down the Champs Elysées, and then he wandered away across Place de la Concorde and entered the Boulevard St. Germain. The clock struck seven as he passed St. Germain des Prés and he hastened his steps, for he had a long way still to go. He turned into one of the small streets near the Jardin des Plantes, and it soon seemed as if he had left Paris behind him. The streets began to darken, and narrowed into lanes, the great shops shrank into small booths, and the cafés became pot-houses. Fine coats became more and more rare, and blouses more numerous. It was nearly eight o'clock, just theatre time down on the brilliant boulevards, and up here groups of workmen wandered home after the day's toil. They looked tired and heavy-hearted, but the work was hard, already by six in the morning the bell was rung in the manufactories and workshops, and many of them had had an hour's walk to come there. Here and there stood a ragged figure with outstretched hand, he carried no inscription on his breast telling how he became blind, he did not recite one word of the story of his misery—he did not need to do that here, for those that gave him a sou were poor themselves, and most of them had known what it meant to be hungry.

The alleys became dirtier and dirtier, and heaps of sweepings and refuse were left in the filthy gutters; it did not matter so much up here where only poor people lived.

The doctor entered an old tumble-down house, and groped his way up the slippery dark stairs as high as he could go. An old woman met him at the door—he was expected. "*Zitto, zitto!*" (hush, hush), said the old woman, with her fingers on her lips; "she sleeps." And in a whisper *la nonna* (the grandmother) reported how things had been going on since yesterday. Raffaella had not been delirious in the night, she had lain quite still and calm the whole day, only now and then she had asked to see the child, and a short while ago she had fallen asleep with the little one in her arms. Did *il signor Dottore* wish to wake her up? No, that he would not do. He sat himself down in silence beside the old woman on the bench. They were very good friends these two, and he knew well the sad story of the family.

They were from St. Germano, the village up amongst the mountains half way between Rome and Naples, whence most of the Italian models came. They had arrived in Paris barely two years ago with a number of men and women from their neighbourhood. Raffaella's mother had caught *la febbre* and died at Hôtel Dieu a couple of months after their arrival, and the old woman and the grandchild had had to look after themselves alone in the foreign city.

And Raffaella had become a model like the others.

And a young artist painted her picture. He painted her beautiful girlish head, he painted her young bosom. And then fell her poor clothes, and he painted her maiden loveliness in its budding spring, in the innocent peace of the sleeping senses. She was the butterfly-winged Psyche, whose lips Eros has not yet kissed; she was Diana's nymph who, tired after hunting, unfastens her chiton and, unseen by mortal eyes, bathes her maiden limbs in the hidden forest lake; she was the fair Dryad of the grove who falls asleep on her bed of flowers.

His last picture was ready. Fame entered the young artist's studio, and a ruined child went out from it.

They separated like good friends, he wrote down her address with a piece of charcoal on the wall, and she went to pose to another painter. So she went from studio to studio, and her innocence protected her no longer.

One day the old grandmother stood humbly at the door of the fashionable studio, and told between her sobs that Raffaella was about to become a mother. Ah yes! he remembered her well, the beautiful girl, and he put some pieces of gold in the old woman's hand and promised to try to do something for her. And he kept his word. The same evening he proposed to his comrades to make a collection for Raffaella's child, and he assumed that there was no one who had a right to refuse. There was no one who had the right to refuse. They all gave what they could, some more and some less, and more than one emptied his purse into the hat which went round for Raffaella's child. They all thought it was such a pity for her, the beautiful girl, to have had such bad luck. They wondered what would become of her, she might of course continue to be a model, but never would she be the same as before. The sculptors all agreed that the beautiful lines of the hip could never stand the trial, and the painters knew well that the exquisite delicacy of her colouring was lost for ever. The child would of course be put out to nurse in the country, and the money collected was enough to pay for a whole year. And it was not a bad idea either to beg their friend, that foreign doctor, who was so fond of Italians, to give an eye to Raffaella, he might perhaps be useful in many future contingencies.

And the doctor, who was so fond of Italians, had often been to see her of late. Raffaella had been so ill, so ill, she had been delirious for days and nights, and this was the first quiet sleep she had had for a long time.

No, the doctor certainly did not wish to wake her up; he sat there in silence beside the old grandmother, deep in thought. He was thinking of Raffaella's story. It was not new to him, that story, the Italian poor quarter had more than once told it him, and he had often enough read it in books. It seemed to him that what he saw in life was far simpler and far sadder than what he read in books. Nor was there in Raffaella's story anything very unusual or very sensational, no great display of feeling either of sorrow or despair, no accusations, no threat for vengeance, no attempt at suicide. Everything had gone so simply in such everyday fashion. It was not with head erect and flaming eyes that the old grandmother had stood before him who was guilty of the child's fall, but in humble resignation she had stopped at the door and sobbed out their misery, and when she left she had prayed the Madonna to reward him for his charity. The poor old woman had her reasons for this— she could not carry her head erect, for life had long since bent her neck under the yoke of daily toil; her eyes could not flame with menace, for they had too often had to beg for bread. She knew not how to accuse, for she herself had been condemned unheard to oppression; she knew not how to demand justice, for life had meant for her one long endurance of wrongs. Her path had lain through darkness and misery, she had seen so little of life's sunlight, and her thoughts had grown so dim under her furrowed brow. She was dull, dull as an old worn-out beast of burden.

And the seducer, he was perhaps after all not more of a blackguard than many others. He had done what he could to atone for a fault, which from his point of view was hardly to be considered so very great, he had provided for a whole year for a child which he said was none of his—what could he do more? He had asked the doctor if he knew of any virtuous models, and the doctor had answered him, "No," for neither did he know of any virtuous models.

And Raffaella had borne her degradation as she had borne her poverty, without bitterness and without despair; she wept sometimes, but she accused no one, neither herself nor him who had injured her. She was resigned. Authors believe that it is so easy to jump into the Seine or to take a dose of laudanum, but it is very difficult. Raffaella was a daughter of the people, no culture had entered into her thought-world, either with its light or its shadow, she was far too natural even to think of such a thing.

He who was cultured had brought forward the question of sending the child into the country or placing it in the *Enfants trouvés* (foundling hospital), and she who was uncultured had known of no other answer than to wind her arms still closer round her child's neck. And *la nonna* (the old grandmother), who scrubbed steps and carried coals all day, and having at last lulled the child to rest in the evening, dead-tired went to sleep with half-shut eyes and a string round her wrist, so as now and then to rock the little one's cradle; neither could she understand that it would be any relief if "*la piccerella*" were to be sent away.

The light fell on the squalid bed, and the doctor looked at his patient. Yes! it was indeed very like her, he certainly was a clever artist that young painter! Her face was only a little paler now, that painful shadow over the forehead was probably not to be seen in the bright studio where the picture was painted, those dark rings round her eyes very likely were not suitable for the Salon. But the same perfection of form in every feature, the same noble shape of the head, the same childishly soft rounding of the cheek, the same curly locks round the beautiful brow; yes, rumour spoke true, she bore the mark of nobility on her forehead, not that of Faubourg St. Germain, but that of Hellas, she bore the features of the Venus of Milo.

It was quite still up there in the dim little garret. The doctor looked at the young mother who slept so peacefully with her child in her arms, he looked at the old woman who sat by his side fingering her rosary. With foreboding sadness he looked into the future which awaited these three, and sorrowfully his thoughts wandered along the way which lay before his poor friends.

Ah yes, Raffaella soon got well, for she was healthy with Nature's youth. Model she never became again, for she could not leave her child. She did not marry, for her people do not forgive one who has had a child by a *Signore*. With the baby at her breast she wandered about in search of work, any work whatever. Her demands were so small, but her chances were still smaller. She found no work. The old woman still held out for a time, then she broke down and Raffaella had to provide food for three mouths. The last savings were gone, and the Sunday clothes were at the pawn-shop. Public charity did not help her, for she was a foreigner, and private charity never came near Raffaella. She had to choose between want or going on the streets. Her child lived and she chose want. The world did not reward her for her choice, for virtue hungers and freezes in the poor quarters of Paris. And she ended like so many others by *fare la Scopa*.[24] Pale and emaciated sat the child on *la nonna's* knee, and with low bent back Raffaella swept the streets where pleasure and luxury went by. Poverty had effaced her beauty, she bore the features of want and hardship. Sorrow had furrowed her brow, but the stamp of nobility was still there. Hats off for virtue in rags! It is greater than the virtue of Faubourg St. Germain!

––––––––––––

Perhaps a clever writer could make a nice little sketch out of Raffaella's story; it is, however, as I said before, neither a very original nor a very exciting one, it is quite commonplace. But I can give you a subject for another little sketch; it is that doctor who is so fond of Italians who has hit upon it. He has been thinking it over for many years, but he never gets further than thinking. Write a story about female models and dedicate it to artists! Write it without lies and without sentimentality. Write it without exaggeration, for it needs none; without severity, for we all have need of forbearance. Tell them, the artists, how much we all like them, the light-hearted good-natured comrades, tell them how proud we are of them, the happy interpreters of our longing for beauty. But ask them why they so despise their models, ask them if they know what becomes of the originals of their female pictures!

They know it well.

If they answer you that they are young, that their temptations are greater than those of any others, then reflect if you yourself have the right to say any more to them. But if they answer you that the fault lies with the models, then tell them to their faces that they lie. Then tell them what road the greater part of the women models take—the statistics are there and they cannot be contradicted. We know well that many of these models have themselves to blame for their misfortunes, but by far the greater part of them owe their fall to the misleading of an artist.

And look here! Is he then quite wrong, that doctor who thinks that the artist stands towards his woman model in the same position as the physician towards his woman patient? Society demands, and is right in demanding, a passionless eye from the physician, and between the physician's respect for his profession and the temptation of the man, honour has no choice. The present day ranks art higher than science, why then is not the artist's respect for his profession great enough to protect a woman model! Why are there no virtuous models? Is not the model the unknown collaborator in the artist's creation, is she not, even she, although unconsciously a humble servant in the temple of art, in that temple where the ancients placed the statue of the chaste Pallas Athene?

Yes, a clever writer may have a good deal more to say about this, and he may also make use of that doctor's meditations if he thinks there is any meaning in them, they have at least the merit of being founded upon experience, experience of the art world of Paris as well as that of Rome.[25]

But he must not forget that it is the spoiled children of our day that he is daring to blame. Should his article be to the point he may be sure he will be very severely censured by them; let him take it as praise for *il n'y a que la vérité qui blesse*! And besides, let him remember that the world's blame is as little worth caring about as its praise.

THE DOGS IN CAPRI

AN INTERIOR

Like the ancient Romans, the Capri dogs devote the greater part of their day to public life. The Piazza is their Forum, and it is there they write their history. When Don Antonio opens the doors of his osteria, and Don Nicolino, barber and bleeder, steps out of his "Salone," Capri begins a new day. From all sides the dogs then come gravely walking forth—the doctor's, the tobacconist's, the secretary's, Don Archangelo's, Don Pietro's, etc. etc., and, after a greeting in accordance with nature's prescribed ceremonial, they seat themselves upon the Piazza to meditate. Don Antonio places a couple of chairs in front of his café, and whilst some of them accept the invitation to lean against them, others prefer the steps leading up to the Church, or that comfortable corner by the Campanile, to whose clock generations have listened with ever-increasing astonishment where, indomitable as the sun, it presses forward on its own path, but alas! not that of the sun.

After a while the dogs from Hotel Pagano make their appearance. They get up later than the others, for they eat a terribly solid dinner. They all descend from the venerable old "Timberio"[26] Pagano, who walks a little behind the rest of his family. Timberio has a cataract in one eye, but the other eye looks out upon life with immovable calm. The Pagano dog-family has always ranked amongst the very first in Capri, and now, since one of their masters, Manfredo, was made Sindaco, they have still further accentuated that reserved bearing which they always understood how to maintain towards the lower orders. They usually form a "circle" of themselves and some of the Liberal dogs in the Municipal Portico. The Conservative dogs, who were beaten at the last election when the Liberal candidate, Manfredo Pagano, became Sindaco, cluster together in a hostile minority on the other side of the Piazza by the steps leading up to the Church. Now and then they take a look inside the Church, and seat themselves down by the door with the greatest decorum, like humble publicans, whilst the Mass is said in the chancel or the *Figlie di Maria* intone the Litany with half-singing voices.

About ten o'clock appear Il Cacciatore's[27] two dogs, mother and son. They go without hesitation straight into Don Antonio's wineshop. They were born upon the island, but they have received an English education, and they well know the taste of a leg of mutton or a piece of roast beef. Don Antonio's dogs have also a certain idea of these things. After several generations a vague Anglicism still survives amongst them from the time when Don Antonio was steward on board an English steamboat, and it is with a visible pride that they say to their Capri colleagues their "Bow-wow-wow—how do you do, sir?" as any stranger approaches their osteria. The German dogs never enter this place; in spite of all Bismarck's efforts to win Don Antonio over to the triple alliance, they are not well looked upon there, their permanent headquarters are still at Morgano's "Zum Hiddigeigei," whence one can hear them barking and yelping till late at night.

The morning passes in calm *dolce far niente* as a preparation for the exertions of the day. Seldom has anything happened since they met here yesterday, seldom is there the slightest indication that the day which now begins will bring in its train any change in the imperturbable harmony of their *status quo*. An Arcadian peace reigns over their whole being, a contemplative calm is stamped upon their faces. And yet this peace hovers over a volcano, like the summer which brightens the slopes of Vesuvius away on the far horizon. Now and then the thunder growls from the depths of Timberio Pagano's broad breast when Hotel Quisisana's shaggy black guardian goes too near him. Seated on each side of the *farmacia* door the two doctors' four-footed assistants stick out their tongues at each other on the sly, and often enough do the dogs of Don Nicolino and Don Chichillo (the new barber) fall upon each other, so that tufts of hair fly around. Animosity, however, soon sinks down again, and, calm as the rippling waves against the old Emperor's bath palace below, the hours glide away in rhythmical monotony.

They watch the girls as they stride past with mighty *Tufa*-stones on their well-poised heads, like the Caryatides of the Erechtheum; they watch the Marina fishermen bringing up for sale in baskets the night's haul of golden *Triglie* and great *Scurmi*, of bright-coloured mussels from some rocky reef, or perhaps a coral-spun old Roman amphora dragged up by the deep *Palamido* nets from out of its thousand-years-old hiding-place at the bottom of the sea.

Sometimes the longing for activity awakes, and they slowly cross the Piazza to the corner of the Anacapri road to gaze dreamily upon the bustling life in front of the stables, where cavalcades of *forestieri* are waiting impatiently whilst saddles are laid upon the donkeys' bleeding backs, and rusty bits are stuffed into their sore mouths. *Aaaaah! Aaaaah! Avanti!!* Off, little donkeys, for Monte Solaro, one hour and a half's stiff climbing with the happy tourists! Yes, the road is beautiful, winding up along the side of the mountain, clad with myrtle and broom. The view widens more and more—*Aaaaah! Aaaaaaaah!!* one more climb, and the vineyards and olive woods lie deep under your feet, and over your head rise steep cliffs as wild in their mighty desolation as the Via Mala of the Alps; and Barbarossa's half-crumbling castle riveted fast upon the edge of the precipice. Beyond gleams the gulf girdled by the immortal beauty of the shore, and from Posilipo's pine-crowned cape, island after island floats away towards the blue distance of the Mediterranean—*wunderbar! kolossal!!*

Under the saddle it burns like fire, and the mouth is so sore with the incessant tugging at the heavy bridle; but courage, little donkey! up above upon the heights lives Padre Anselmo in his hermit chapel, and he has good wine for thirsty throats!

Other dogs who do not get so far as the donkey-stand lean thoughtfully against the parapet of the Piazza, where some lounging sailors look out over the gulf. The eyes wander far over the gleaming line of Naples, and the mighty silhouette of Vesuvius, or follow absently the direction of some outstretched hand pointing towards Capo Sorrento, whence can be seen the steamboat on its way to Capri. And here come the two blind old men, Fenocchio and Giovanni, groping their way across the Piazza to their usual corner at the edge of the path, where the hum of thousands of gay tourists has rustled by them, where they have sat for so many years with their old fisher-caps in outstretched hands, and their vacant eyes staring into their eternal night of gleaming sunshine: "*Date u soldo Eccellenza al povero cieco! La Madonna vi accompagna!*"

Up on the Piazza the dogs are beginning to awake, and in scattered groups they wander across to the parapet to stare at the steamboat which glides past in the blue water on its way to the Grotto. It is time to start down to the Marina to greet the arriving strangers. Quisisana's, Pagano's, and Hôtel de France's dogs solemnly escort their respective porters to the arched entrance of the Piazza with its Bourbon coat-of-arms still enthroned above it. Small ready-saddled donkeys also clatter patiently down the old stairway to the Marina, and with loud cracks of the whip Felicello's coachmen rattle down the new carriage-road. From the Piazza above, they watch the steamer anchoring outside the harbour, and the small boats landing the passengers. A faint interest lights up the passive faces of the lookers-on when the first strangers reach the Piazza. But alas! always the same invariable types, always the same colossal matron on the same slender little donkey, always the same correct "misses" in Felicello's landau, always the same fiery-red noisy Germans, wrangling over prices with the girls who have dragged their boxes up the heights to the town. Seldom are there any dogs amongst the arrivals, seldom does any occasion whatever arise for interference in one way or another—passivity, nothing but passivity!

Now the hotel bells ring for luncheon, and they one and all wander home. The processes of digestion are carried out, according to correct physiological laws undisturbed by any brain-work, and the afternoon is passed in a siesta on some loggia, whilst the sun's rays slowly climb the Anacapri cliff, and long shadows begin to glide down Monte Solaro's slopes towards the town. The air is cool and refreshing, and they prepare to resume public business on the Piazza. The second event of the day is about to happen. The post arrives. Don Peppino (post-master) solemnly shuts his office-door, and the loiterers wait with interest whilst the post-bag is being opened inside. Always the same disappointment—no letters for them, all the letters and newspapers are for the strangers in the hotels! Sometimes they get hold of a *Corriere di Napoli* or a *Pungolo*, and then they disappear into some corner by themselves to make people believe that they can read; but after they have devoured the whole newspaper they are none the wiser for it. So they become drowsy again and wander a few times round the Piazza, past Don Antonio's *osteria* with the faded photographs and dried-up biscuits in the window, and a few unconscious philosophers meditating inside; past Il Salone, where the flies keep watch over Don Nicolino's dreams; past La Farmacia, where the morphia of idleness soothes Don Petruccio's ideas to rest; past the stables where the donkeys are pushed into their dark holes after the strangers have returned from their expedition. They look out over the gulf where Ischia blushes in fading sunlight, while dark-blue twilight falls around Vesuvius. The day's session draws to an end and the Piazza is becoming deserted. Up in the Campanile there suddenly breaks out a terrible row amongst the cogs and wheels, and at last the old machinery loses its temper altogether, and, getting hold of a rusty hammer, begins to beat with all its might on some unwilling bells: "*Ventiquattro ore*," yawns Don Nicolino, shutting up his Salone; "*Ventiquattro ore*," say the flies, and go to sleep amongst the brushes and combs; "*Ventiquattro ore*," say the dogs, and go home with the feeling of having performed their duty to gather strength for the next day's toils by twelve or fourteen hours' dreamless sleep.

Then the church bells ring out the Ave Maria, and the day sinks into the sea.

So passes day after day, each like the other, as are the beads of the rosaries which glide between the fingers of the *Figlie di Maria* inside the Church. Each morning collects the citizens for social duty on the Piazza—each evening the campanile exhorts them to go to rest.

Under the walls of the houses the shadows begin to grow smaller and smaller, and the paving-stones of the Piazza get hotter and hotter in the sun-bath. Uneasy dreams begin to disturb the peace of the siesta, and Capri is seized with an irresistible desire to scratch itself. Don Antonio spreads the awning before his wineshop, and the questions of the day are oftener and oftener dealt with under its protecting shade. They linger later on the Piazza in the warm evenings, and with nose in the air they sit for long hours on the parapet looking out over the gulf towards Vesuvius, whose mighty smoke-cloud slowly spreads over the mainland—the wind is south, all is as it should be! And, with apprehensive thoughts of fatigues to come, they troop home to their much-needed repose.

The Piazza is quite empty, now and then a short bark is heard from some wineshop, or a howling "*Potz Donner Wetter!*" from Hiddigeigei's beer-house, then everything is still, and only the old watchman in the Campanile counts over the hours of the night in a sonorous brazen voice to keep himself awake. Still for a while the white town gleams out amongst the cliffs, then it becomes quite dark and Capri's isle sinks into the gloom of night.

But lo! already climbs the moon over Sorrento's mountain, and the veil of twilight glides down Monte Solaro's heights, over shimmering olive woods, over orange and myrtle groves, and vanishes amid the waves of the gulf. Night dreams a beautiful dream, and mysteriously the siren's moonlit island rises out of the dark sea. A gentle south wind breathes over the water, murmurs amidst the half-slumbering waves, flies fragrantly over orange-trees in blossom, and playfully rocks the tender vine branches. Jubilant voices call out from the sea, louder and louder they sound in the stillness of the night, and the wanderer on Monte Solaro hears the rustling of wings in the moonlit space above.

When Capri awakes the next morning, every one knows that the wild geese have passed. Spring has come, and the shooting season has begun! From early morning the Piazza is full of dogs. The quiet of everyday life has departed, a certain energy animates their dull features, and the reflection of an idea lights up the contemplative gloom of their eyes.

In front of Maria Vacca's butcher-shop hangs a dead quail, and outside Don Antonio's *osteria* stand guns in long rows, and upon the chairs lie great game-bags and powder-horns. Il Cacciatore has been in the wineshop since sunrise, in colossal shooting-boots with cartridge-belt round his waist. Woe to the quail which may now appear in Maria Vacca's shop! It vanishes at once into Il Cacciatore's game-bag. Inside the Municipal Portico a younger generation listens to old Timberio Pagano's shooting stories of the days of his youth, when many thousand quails were caught in a day, and up on the Church steps the clericals think sadly of that period of vanished splendour when Capri had its own Bishop, whose maintenance was paid by the quail harvest—"*Vescovo delle quaglie*"[28] as he was called in Rome. Excitement increases as the hours pass, and when at last the Campanile's bells announce that the first day's shooting is over, each one goes to his home to gather strength for the next day's exertions. Once again darkness falls upon the island, and Capri sleeps the sleep of the just.

On tired wings swarms of birds fly over the sea. Thousands have fallen on Africa's coasts, where they assembled for their long journey, thousands have sunk exhausted amidst the waves, thousands will die on the rocky island which glimmers from afar in the darkness. Sheltered by the last hour of gloom they approach the island and silently swoop down upon its steep coast, upon the heights by Villa di Tiberio, where the hermit watches behind his snares; amongst the cliffs of Mitromania and the Piccola Marina, where nets are spread to catch their wings; upon the headlands of Limbo and Punta di Carena, where the Capri dogs, stealthy as cats, sneak round after their prey. When day dawns over Monte Solaro, and its first rays stream even as they did two thousand years ago in sacred fire upon the old sun-god's crumbling altar in the grotto of Mitromania,[29] hundreds of birds, quails, wood-pigeons, larks, thrushes, flutter in the nets around, and hundreds of others bleed to death amongst the cliffs—but what cares the sun for that! What matters it to the sun that the darkness he disperses conceals a multitude of worn-out birds from rapacious eyes, that to-day death stalks from cliff to cliff along the track shown by his gleaming light:

"So che Natura è sorda, Che miserar non sa; Che non del Ben sollecita Fu, ma dell 'esser solo."[30]

Upon the heights of Monte Solaro sits Il Cacciatore, armed to the teeth, looking with the eye of a conqueror over the field of battle below. The day has been a hot one, Il Cacciatore has fired some hundred shots in different directions. At his feet lie his two dogs, mother and son, and behind him sits Spadaro with an extra gun in his hands and an enormous game-bag over his shoulder. Now and then mother and son give little yelps and wag their tails, following in their dreams an escaping bird, now and then Il Cacciatore's hand fumbles after his trusty gun to bring down an imaginary quail or pigeon, now and then Spadaro seems to stuff some new booty into his vast bag. Deeper and deeper grows the silence over Monte Solaro. Down at their feet the three rocks of Faraglione shine in purple and gold, and the glow of the sinking sun falls on the waves of the gulf. From the town of Capri hotel bells ring for dinner. A fragrant hallucination of quail-pie tickles Il Cacciatore's nostrils, and from under his half-shut eyelids the whole gulf assumes a tantalising resemblance to a sea of pure *Capri rosso*—that purple hue which already old Homer likened to red wine—whilst Spadaro's more modest imagination hears the macaroni splutter and boil in the murmur of the waves against the cliff below, and sees the purple glow of the evening sun pour masses of "pumaroli"[31] sauce over it.

Suddenly Il Cacciatore rubs his eyes and looks dreamily around, and Spadaro investigates with amazement the bag, where only a single little lark, which was on its way to give spring concerts in the north, sleeps his last sleep. *Hallo! Spadaro! Andiamonci!*[32] The dogs wake up by degrees, and the caravan starts slowly on its way towards Capri. Tired by the day's toil, at last they reach the Piazza and its friendly wineshop, where Il Cacciatore sits down to rest whilst Spadaro and the dogs carry home the lark in triumph.

So pass the weeks of the shooting season in continued exertions. Every morning before daybreak they start off to try and capture Spring in its flight, every evening they meet on the Piazza to rest, and often enough do we assemble round our friend Il Cacciatore's table to partake of a magnificent quail-pie, such as only he can put before us.

But although the ranks are thinned, the March of The Ten Thousand still advances victoriously. Soon the larks sing over the frosty fields in the distant North, soon the swallows twitter under the eaves of the far-off little cottage, which has lain so long half-buried in snow, and the quails sound their monotonous note in the spring evenings.

The shooting season is over, and the Capri dogs sit blankly upon the Piazza, staring out over the gulf in the direction the bird flew when he escaped out of their hands. Higher and higher the sacred fire flames each morning upon the sun-god's altar down in Mitromania's grotto, brighter and brighter the Faraglioni rocks gleam each evening with purple and gold, with a still ruddier glow the wine-hue of the gulf fascinates Il Cacciatore's retina. Silently the liberal dogs ponder over the burning questions of the day, and, panting, the clericals listen from their sunny church steps to the prophecies of the fires of *Il purgatorio*, which the priests proclaim every Sunday inside the cool Church. Public life ceases by degrees, and it seems as if a reaction sets in after the excitement of the shooting season. The arrival of the steamer is certainly still watched from the Piazza, and with one eye open they look at the few strangers who wander up to the Piazza with outspread sketching-umbrellas and easel and colour-box on a boy's head. True, they still assemble in front of the closed door of the office to await the opening of the post-bag, but interest in political life has slackened, and their hope of letters has become a quiet resignation. Inside the *Farmacia* the drugs ferment in their pots, and in Don Nicolino's Salone living frescoes of flies adorn the walls. About the slopes of Monte Salaro the Scirocco hangs in heavy clouds, and an irresistible drowsiness settles down upon the Piazza. Capri enters into its summer torpor.

When it awakes the sun has subdued his fire, and the table stands ready spread for the lords of creation to seat themselves and feast, and for the dogs to gather up the fragments that remain. From the *pergola* over their heads hang grapes in heavy clusters, and amidst the shade of the orange-groves peep out juicy figs and red-cheeked peaches. Then comes the Bacchanalia of the vintage, with song and jest and maiden's bright eyes looking out from under huge baskets of grapes, and naked feet freeing the slumbering butterfly of wine from its crushed chrysalis.

Over the Piazza a cooling sea breeze blows now and again, and Capri takes a refreshing bath of heavy autumnal rain to wash away the heat and dust of summer. The dogs save themselves in time from the vivacity of the unknown element, but millions of obscure lives are drowned in the streams which force their way like a deluge over the bloody battle-field of summer, whilst others find their Ararat amongst the brushes in Don Nicolino's Salone.

The mist of unconsciousness is gradually lifted from the dogs' brains, and waking dreams about activity and strength stare out from their half-shut eyes. Don Nicolino smilingly dusts the halo of flies from his portrait, and, deep in thought, Don Petruccio composes a new elixir of life from summer's *mixtum compositum*. Fenocchio and Giovanni seat themselves again in their corner to wash a little copper out of the tourist stream, and with trembling legs the small donkeys once more unload numbers of *forestieri* in the Piazza. From Vesuvius the smoke falls in long cloud-streamers over the gulf, and upon the wings of the Tramontana (the north wind), Summer flies home again after her wedding-trip to the North. In vain do the Capriotes spread their nets once more round the shores of the island; in vain do the dogs lie in wait amongst the rocks; in vain does Il Cacciatore sit in full armour on the heights of Monte Solaro and shoot off his cartridges after the fugitive—Summer passes by.

With drooping tails the dogs sit huddled together upon the stones of their Piazza, thinking with sorrow of their departed summer idyll. From snow-covered Apennines, Winter comes sailing in his foam-hidden dragon-ship over the uneasy waters of the gulf. The storm thunders amidst the ruins of the old watch-tower, whose alarm-bell[33] has been silent for so long, and amongst the foaming breakers the mad Viking boards Capri's cliffs. Strong as a whirlwind he cuts in pieces the pergola garlands which were left hanging after Autumn's Bacchanalian feast, and, brutal as a savage, he tears asunder the leaf-woven chiton which clothed the Dryad of the grove.

But down in Mitromania's grotto the sacred fire flames as before upon the old Persian god's altar, and tenderly the God of Day spreads his shining shield over his beloved island and bids the barbarian from the North go to sea again. So he departs, the rough stranger, his errand unaccomplished, without having robbed a single rose from the maiden's sun-warmed cheek, without having stolen a single golden fruit from the everlasting green of the orange groves. And scarcely has he turned his back before tiny fearless violets peep carefully out from among the hillocks, and narcissus and rosemary clamber high up on the steep cliffs to see whither the harsh Northerner has gone, and soon a whole flock of flower children come and set themselves down to play at summer in the grass.

Upon the Piazza the dogs sit as before in sunny contemplation. The cycle of their life's emotions has been run through, and they begin to turn over anew the blank pages of their history, page after page in unvarying sequence. Day follows day and year follows year, and soon old age comes and scatters some white almond blossom upon their heads. The buoyant delights of the senses are benumbed, youth's far-flying thoughts have broken their wings against the four walls of the Piazza, and like tame ducks they go round and round their enclosed space, from Don Antonio's wineshop to Felicello's donkey-stand, from Don Nicolino's Salone to Don Petruccio's Farmacia. Now and again the free cry of the passing wild geese high above in space reaches the Piazza, the early youthful courage wakes anew, and they sluggishly tramp along towards the Anacapri road as far as their heavy limbs can carry them. Now and again a faint echo from some world's revolution trembles on their tympanums through Don Peppino's post-office, and they look away in dreaming peace to the white town of Naples, the noise of whose human life is lost amidst the murmur of the waves, or away to the old revolutionist Vesuvius, whose threatening wrath will never reach their Eden.

So they sit on their Piazza, staring out upon the river of time as it flows past them. They still sit there staring for a few more years to come, then they move no more—they have become hypnotised. The struggle for existence has ceased, and imperceptibly they sink into Buddha's Nirvâna, unconscious, painless, inebriate with the sun.

ZOOLOGY

They say that love for mankind is the highest of all virtues. I admire this love for mankind, and I know well that it only belongs to noble minds. My soul is too small, my thought flies too near the earth ever to reach so far, and I am obliged to acknowledge that the longer I live the farther I depart from this high ideal. I should lie if I said that I love mankind.

But I love animals, oppressed, despised animals, and I do not care when people laugh at me because I say that I feel happier with them than with the majority of people I come across.

When one has spoken with a human being for half an hour, one has, as a rule, had quite enough, isn't it so? I, at least, then usually feel inclined to slip away, and I am always astonished that he with whom I have been speaking has not tried to escape long before. But I am never bored in the society of a friendly dog, even if I do not know him or he me. Often when I meet a dog walking along by himself, I stop and ask him where he is going and have a little chat with him; and even if no further conversation takes place, it does me good to look at him and try to enter into the thoughts which are working in his mind. Dogs have this immense advantage over man that they cannot dissimulate, and Talleyrand's paradox that speech has been given us in order to conceal our thoughts, cannot at all be applied to dogs.

I can sit half the day in a field watching the grazing cattle; and to observe the physiognomy of a little donkey is one of the keenest pleasures of a psychologist. But it is specially when donkeys are free that they are most interesting, a tied-up donkey is not nearly so communicative as when she is loose and at liberty, and that after all is not much to be wondered at.

At Ischia I lived for a long time almost exclusively with a donkey. It was Fate which brought us together. I lived in a little boat-house down at the Marina, and the donkey lived next door to me. I had quite lost my sleep up in the stifling rooms of the hotel, and had gladly accepted my friend Antonio's invitation to live down at the Marina in his cool boat-house, while he was out fishing in the bay of Gaeta. I fared exceedingly well in there amongst the pots and fishing-nets; and astride on the keel of an old upturned boat I wrote long love-letters to the sea. And when evening came and it began to grow dusk in the boat-house, I went to bed in my hammock, with a sail for a covering and the memory of a happy day for a pillow. I fell asleep with the waves and I woke with the day. Each morning came my neighbour, the old donkey, and stuck in her solemn head through the open door, looking steadfastly at me. I always wondered why she stood there so still and did nothing but stare at me, and I could not hit upon any other explanation than that she thought I was nice to look at. I lay there half awake looking at her—I thought that she too was nice to look at. She resembled an old family portrait as she stood there with her gray head framed by the doorway against the blue background of a summer's morning. Out there it grew lighter and lighter, and the clear surface of the sea began to glitter. Then came a ray of sunlight dancing right into my eyes, and I sprang up and greeted the gulf. I had nothing whatever to do all day, but the poor donkey was supposed to be at work the whole forenoon up in Casamicciola. There grew, however, such a sympathy between us that I found a substitute for her, and then we wandered carelessly about all day long, like true vagabonds wherever the road led us. Sometimes it was I who went first with the donkey trotting quietly at my heels, sometimes it was she who had got a fixed determination of her own, and then I naturally followed her. I studied the whole time with great attention the interesting personality I had so unexpectedly come across, and it was long since I had found myself in such congenial company. I might have much more to say about all this, but these psychological researches may prove far too serious a topic for many of my readers, and I therefore believe I had better stop here.

And the birds, who can ever tire of them? Hour after hour I can sit on a mossy stone and listen to what a dear little bird has to say—I, who can never keep my thoughts together when some one is talking to me. But have you noticed how sweet a little bird is to look at when he sings his song, and now and again bends his graceful head, as if to listen for some one to answer far away in the forest? In the late summer, when the bird-mother has to teach her children to talk—do not believe it is only a matter of instinct, even they have to take lessons in learning their singing language—have you watched these lessons when the mother from her swinging-chair lectures about something or other, and the summer-old little ones stammer after her with their clear child-voices?

And when the birds are silent, I have only to look down among the grass and moss to light on other acquaintances to keep me company. Over waving grass and corn flies a dragon-fly on wings of sun-glitter and fairy-web, and deep down in the path, which winds between the mighty grass stems, a little ant struggles on with a dry fir-needle on her back. Rough is the road, now it goes up-hill and now it goes down-hill, now she pushes the heavy load like a sledge before her, now she carries it upon her slender shoulders. She pulls so hard up-hill that her whole little body stiffens, she rolls down the steep slopes with her burden clasped tightly in her arms; but she never lets go, and onward it goes, for the ant is in a hurry to get home. Soon the dew will fall, and then it is unsafe to be out in the trackless forest, and best to be home in peace after the day's work is ended. Now the road becomes mountainous and steep, and suddenly a mighty rock rises in front of her—what the name of that rock is the ant knows well enough; I know nothing, and to me it looks like an ordinary pebble. The ant stops short and ponders awhile, then she gives a signal with her antennæ, which I am too stupid to understand but which others at once respond to, for from behind a dry leaf I see two other ants approach to the rescue. I watch how they hold a council of war, and how the new arrivals with great concern pull the log to try how heavy it is. Suddenly they stand quite still and listen—an ant-patrol marches by a little way off, and I see how a couple of ants are told off to lend assistance. Then they all take hold together, and like sailors they haul up the log with a long slow pull.

I understand it is to repair the havoc made by an earthquake that the log is to be used—how many hard-working lives were perhaps crushed under the ruins of the fallen houses, and what evil power was it that destroyed what so much patient labour built up? I dare not ask, for who knows if it were not a passing man who amused himself by knocking down the ant-hill with his stick!

And all the other tiny creatures, whose name I do not know, but into whose small world I look with joy, they also are fellow-citizens in Creation's great society, and probably they fulfil their public duties far better than I fulfil mine!

And besides, when thus lying down and staring into the grass, one ends by becoming so very small oneself.

And at last it seems to me as if I were nothing but an ant myself, struggling on with my heavy load through the trackless forest. Now it goes up-hill and now it goes down-hill. But the thing is not to let go. And if there is some one to help to give a pull where the hill seems too steep and the load too heavy, all goes well enough.

But suddenly Fate comes passing by and knocks down all that has been built up with so much hard labour.

The ant struggles on with her heavy load deep in the trackless forest. The way is long, and there is still some time before the day's work is over and the dew falls.

But high overhead flies the dream on wings of sun-glitter and fairy-web.

HYPOCHONDRIA

The study of micro-organisms has directed medical science into new channels, and thrown open a hitherto undreamt-of world for eager investigators. The list of recent discoveries in bacteriology is already a long one. Koch's researches in cholera and tuberculosis, and Pasteur's method of vaccination against hydrophobia, are but links in the chain which one day shall fetter the hydra-headed dragon of disease. Less known, but hardly less important, are the very latest studies of hypochondria, which have led to the discovery that this evil also belongs to infectious diseases.

Struck by the constant disorder of thought and sensibility which characterise the hypochondriac, the doctors have up till now placed this malady amongst the nervous diseases, and it is in the central organs of the nervous system, more especially the brain, that its seat and origin have been determined. We finally know that hypochondria is an infectious disease, caused by a microbe which has been isolated, and named *Bacillus niger* (A. M.).

It is after all astonishing that this discovery has escaped so many investigators ever since Burton, whose *Anatomy of Melancholy* still remains unparalleled—it is astonishing when one considers the many analogies which connect this so-called nervous disease with some of the best-known bacterial diseases, such as hydrophobia, tuberculosis, and cholera. As in hydrophobia, so in hypochondria the virus spreads over the nervous system, produces constant and well-known disorders in the brain, and ends here also by paralysis, paralysis of the affected individual's intellectual and moral functions, and, at last, mental death. As in hydrophobia, one also notices by the bacillus niger infection cramp in certain groups of muscles—that of the muscles of laughter being, for instance, very common. This cramp, *risus sardonicus*, is excessively painful, and its prognostic signification is a bad one, for it is a characteristic of absolutely incurable cases (Heine).

The tendency to bite, which characterises hydrophobia, is also encountered in certain forms of hypochondria (Schopenhauer). As a rule the affected individual is, however, inoffensive and resigned (Leopardi).

The cholera characteristic, *Stadium algidum*, is also to be found in bacillus niger infection—a Stadium algidum when the soul slowly grows cold, and at last reaches the zero of insensibility (Tiberius).

The curious, and, up till now, unexplained immunity which protects certain individuals from cholera, appears again in hypochondria—so, for instance, have idiots shown themselves absolutely refractory, *i.e.* not receptive of the bacillus niger infection. The explanation of the relative rarity of hypochondria is probably to be found in this fact. . . .

In analogy with what experimental pathology has taught us about the microbes of cholera and tuberculosis, the bacillus niger does not seem to thrive on animals, though several exceptions to this rule are to be found, and as the tuberculosis bacillus is exceedingly common amongst cows, so may be pointed out the great diffusion of bacillus niger infection amongst old donkeys (Rosina). I do not believe, though, that here, as with the cows, one can speak of spontaneous infection—the virus has, in the case of the old donkey, more probably been introduced into the blood through a flogged back. Dogs seem, after a long contact with infected individuals, to be receptive of contagion (Puck).

Bacillus niger originates in the heart—there is no doubt about that—the disorders of the brain are secondary. The explanation why the seat of the evil has been supposed to be the brain is natural enough, because as a rule it is only since the infection has spread to the brain that the malady can be diagnosed. So long as bacillus niger has only attacked the heart, the diagnosis is much more difficult. The nature of the evil can, however, here, as in certain forms of tuberculosis, be easily enough detected at the back of the eyes. This is probably in relation with the morbid alteration of the organ of sight, which characterises the bacillus niger infection—*the patient sees life as it is*; when, on the contrary, as is well known, in the normal eye the vision of the outer world is reflected through certain media, illusions and never-dying hope, before it is transferred through the optic nerve to the brain.

As with microbes of the before-mentioned diseases, bacillus niger is also exceedingly tenacious of life. Its virulence can be temporarily reduced by alcohol, ink, and music. As for alcohol, its effect is indubitable, but unfortunately of very short duration. The microbe very soon—indeed, already the next morning, according to all experimentalists—regains its full vigour, and its temporary inactivity seems rather to have increased its virulence instead of decreasing it. Like most of the other antimicrobic agents, alcohol is in itself a deadly poison, and its application in the treatment of the disease is therefore very limited. It is to be used with the greatest precaution, for there are numerous instances of the individual having followed his microbe to the grave.

May I here mention *en passant* a harmless old quack remedy—the common practice of smoking out the microbe. The home of the tobacco-plant is the same land where the poppy of oblivion blossoms, the silent shores between which flows the stream of Lethe. The fragrance of its leaf has deadened the microbe in more than one diseased brain, the clouds from an old pipe have hidden the reality from more than one sorrowful eye. (Do you remember Rodolphe in Henri Murger's *Vie de Bohème*?)

Ink as a bactericide is less known, but worth consideration. I know of a case, to which I shall return later, where a momentary amelioration was produced by an ink-cure. Contrary to alcohol, this specific can be used without any danger whatever to the individual himself—the danger being limited to his surroundings. The microbe is dipped in the ink-stand, and fixed on paper to dry. It maintains, however, its virulence long enough, and can, transplanted in a fertile soil, regain its vigour and grow. The preparation must, therefore, be strictly locked up in the writing-desk, which now and then must be disinfected, the surest disinfectant being here, as always, fire.

As for music, this treatment was known even in the childhood of science; it was already highly esteemed by the ancients—hypochondria is, as is well known, one of the oldest of all diseases; it resounds already in the choruses of Sophocles and Euripides. The new world of bacteriology was then undreamt of, but the discoveries of thousands of years have done no more than verify the experience of the ancients. Music still remains the greatest consoler of sorrow-stricken man. Still to-day Saul seeks relief for his sombre soul from David's harp, still to-day does Orpheus conquer the shades of Hades by the sound of his lute; still to-day the song calls out for the Eurydice of our longing.

As was to be expected, the discovery of the microbe of hypochondria gave quite a new direction to the study of the treatment of this disease. To relate here the far-reaching experiences which followed the isolation of the bacillus niger would carry us too far—enough to say that the results of these investigations have unfortunately up till now been hopelessly negative. We, however, find it expedient to mention in a few words the experiments in air-therapeutics by which the discoverer of the microbe hoped to find a remedy for the evil—true that the result was even here negative, but there is a certain amount of interest still attached to these experiments which, pursued with more patience, might perhaps have led to a more satisfactory result. Starting from the analogy between the bacillus niger infection and tuberculosis, the doctor emitted his hypothesis of a region of immunity from hypochondria as well as from consumption, of a possibility of finding in the pure air of the high altitudes a medium where the development of bacillus niger in the mind would cease, as well as the development of the tuberculosis-bacilli in the lungs. It was in the domain of experimental pathology—the field where Pasteur and Koch reaped their laurels—that the solution of the problem was to be looked for, and the bacterium in question living almost exclusively on mankind, the suitable animal for experiment had in this case necessarily to be a man. The doctor had for several years attended an individual affected with the complaint in question. It was a fine case. We quote here from the notes of the doctor: "Man about thirty. The patient maintains an obstinate silence as to the origin of his sufferings; it is, however, evident that the evil dates from several years back. External examination nothing remarkable—on the contrary. Big dog at his heels. Energy but little developed. Active impulses wanting. Ambition rudimentary. Intelligence mediocre—maybe slightly above. Sense of humour well defined, as usual in these cases. Sensibility abnormally developed. Heart perhaps rather large. Tendency for idealism. Patient has hallucinations—fancies, for instance, he is surrounded by people who suffer and hunger; imagines seeing all sorts of animals oppressed and tortured to death." The doctor had in vain prescribed several things in order to calm and distract his diseased mind, rest-cure in Anacapri for a whole year; earthquake in Ischia, cholera in Naples, etc. etc., but without any enduring result. Returned to Paris, the patient had, though with visible aversion, gone through a cure of ink-treatment, and in the beginning had felt a little better for it, but had soon fallen back to his normal condition of hopeless dejection. The doctor was at his wit's end, and began to be bored to death by the continual lamentations of his patient. The unfortunate man was perpetually hanging about in the doctor's consulting-room, and ended by taking up nearly his whole day, to the great detriment of his other practice. It was then the doctor communicated to his patient his hypothesis of the possibility of a region of immunity from hypochondria, as from consumption, and the desirability of finding a fitting animal for experiment, for the purpose of studying the influence of high altitudes on hypochondria.

The patient placed himself at the doctor's absolute disposal.

On the top of Mont Blanc (4810 mètres) the doctor still found a considerable quantity of microbes in the thoughts of his patient. The patient complained that he felt so small and forlorn up there on the pinnacles of Nature's temple, where all around him the Alps raised their marble-shining arch of triumph over the silent cloud-heavy earth. With awe he bent his eyes before the beaming majesty of the sun, where, indomitable and unconscious, the Almighty Ruler trod his course over the shade and light of the valleys, over the sorrow and joy of man.

Chained to the ice-axe firmly riveted in the frozen snow, did the doctor leave his patient for a whole night on a projecting rock, under the shoulder of the Matterhorn (4273 mètres), while the snowstorm passed. Now and then a flash of lightning flamed through the icy night of the desolate precipices; like combating Titans, giant-shaped crags stood out between storm-driven clouds, and the mighty mountain shook, while the thunder rolled over the snow-fields. Then everything became still; the storm passed by, and like silent birds of the night heavy flakes of snow floated through the darkness. With stiff-frozen limbs, half-covered with snow, sat the patient in mute wonder, looking out over Matterhorn's sombre cliffs, over Monte Rosa's desolate glaciers. The patient complained of feeling so utterly helpless before the magnificent force which had built up this, the proudest monument of the Alps, so crushed before the time-defying Titan, who, it seemed to him, was only going to fall with the world, which was his footstool. . . . He listened with awe to the mountains answer; high above his head he heard the thunder of loosening rocks, and while the echo replied from the Ebihorn cliffs, an avalanche of rattling stones rolled along the flank of the mountain to break into fragments and disappear deep down amongst the crevices of the Zmutt glacier—mute testimonies that even the mightiest mountain of the Alps was condemned to crumble away into grains of sand in the hour-glass of the Eternal, broken fragments from the oldest monument of creation, teaching, like the modern hieroglyphics from the Nile, that all shall perish.

As the night passed on the patient felt more and more downcast and miserable. The doctor had already given up the experiment as hopeless, when towards daybreak, to his great astonishment, symptoms of an unmistakable amelioration showed themselves. The patient's head had fallen on the guide's shoulder; a painless repose crept over his stiffening limbs, and with utmost interest the doctor found an almost complete absence of bacillus niger in the benumbed thought of his patient. The doctor watched for a while in great excitement the patient's pale face, while the darkness of the night vanished more and more, and the dawn of a new day flew over the horizon. He was just going to make a new test on bacillus niger, when one of the guides suddenly leaned his ear against the patient's breast, and then anxiously began to rub his nostrils and half-open eyelids with brandy, and to pull his arms and legs. . . .

When he shortly afterwards slowly opened his eyes, he was more depressed than ever, and remained decidedly worse for several days.

After renewed experiments on Monte Rosa, Schreckhorn, Die Jungfrau, and a prolonged observation in a crevasse under the Mont Maudit cliffs of Mont Blanc (1471 mètres), the doctor had to give up his hypothesis of immunity from hypochondria. In spite of the isolation of the microbe, we are obliged to admit that no positive result has been gained up till now as to the treatment of the affected individual—the analogy with cholera and even tuberculosis can, alas! be applied even here. We continue to remain powerless to cure hypochondria. We are able to soothe the sufferings of the hypochondriac, because we are able to deaden his microbe—kill it, we cannot. After more or less time the bacillus niger recovers his virulence, and the diseased individual retakes his momentary interrupted course towards the sombre land whence no traveller returns, and over whose doors are written those words of the great seer:

"Lasciate ogni Speranza, voi ch'entrate!"

A severe scientific critic might, however, object that the above-mentioned experiment on the influence of high altitude on hypochondria was not pursued long enough to make its negative result absolutely conclusive. Who knows if the solution of the problem did not slip out of the doctor's hands that night on the Matterhorn? Who knows if the patient might not for all time have been freed from his bacillus, if he had been allowed to remain a little longer up there on the Matterhorn's cliff, under the cover of the falling snow, while the darkness of the night vanished more and more from his benumbed thought, and the dawn of a new day flew past his half-opened eye?

LA MADONNA DEL BUON CAMMINO

The doctor had often seen him at the door of the sanctuary looking out over the dirty lane, and, even when a long distance from each other, friendly salutations were exchanged between them in the usual Neapolitan fashion of waving hands, with "*Buon giorno, Don Dionisio!*" "*Ben venuto, Signor Dottore!*"

Often, too, he had looked in at the old deserted cloister garden, with its dried-up fountain and a few pale autumn roses against the wall of the little chapel. And Don Dionisio had related to him many of the miracles of the Madonna of Buon Cammino. The Madonna of Buon Cammino stood there quite alone in her half-ruined sanctuary, and only one tiny little oil-lamp struggled with the darkness within. With great solemnity Don Dionisio had drawn aside the curtain which veiled his Madonna from profane eyes; and tenderly as a mother he had arranged the tattered fringes of her robe, which threatened to fall to pieces altogether. And the doctor had looked with compassionate wonder upon the pale waxen image with the impassive smile on the rigid features, which to Don Dionisio's eyes reflected the highest physical and spiritual beauty. "*Come è bella, come è simpatica!*"[34] said he, looking up at his Madonna.

Inside the old church of Santa Maria del Carmine, close by, hundreds of votive candles were burning before the altars, and night and day the people flocked in there to implore the mighty Madonna's protection. Mothers took the rings off their hands and hung them as sacred offerings round the Madonna's neck, girls drew the strings of coral out of their dark plaits to adorn the rich robe of the statue, and, with brows pressed against the worn marble floor, strong men knelt, murmuring prayers for help and mercy.

Death dwelt in the slums of Naples. Three times the wonder-working image of the Madonna del Carmine had been carried round the quarter in solemn procession to protect the people of the Mercato from the dreaded plague, and many miracles were reported of dying people brought back to life on being permitted to kiss the hem of the garment of the blessed Maria del Carmine.

The doctor had seen Don Dionisio disappear into his little portico with a disdainful shrug when the procession of Maria del Carmine passed by, and he had more than once heard the old priest express his doubts about the far-famed Madonna's wonder-working power to one gossip or another, whom he had succeeded in stopping on her way to the church of the Madonna.

"What, after all, has your Madonna done for you, you people of Mercato?" he called out mockingly. "If she is so powerful, why has she not saved Naples from the cholera? And here, in the midst of her own quarter in Mercato, whose inhabitants for centuries have knelt before her, what has she done to prevent the disease spreading here? Do not people die every day round her own sanctuary, round the very Piazza del Mercato, in spite of all your prayers, in spite of all your votive candles? *Altro che la Madonna del Carmine!*[35]

"And as the cholera has never reached this side of the Piazza, and never will reach it, whom do you suppose you have to thank for that, if not the holy Madonna del Buon Cammino, who stretches her protecting hand over you although you do not deserve it, although you leave her sanctuary dark and take all your offerings to the other Madonnas, whatever their names may be! And yet you cannot see in your blindness that the blessed Madonna del Buon Cammino is far more powerful than all your Madonnas put together! *Altro che la Madonna del Carmine!*"

But no one seemed to take any heed of the old man's words, no votive candles dispersed the darkness within the chapel of the blessed Madonna del Buon Cammino, and no lips murmured her name in their prayers for help and protection against the dreaded sickness. Had they not Santa Maria del Carmine close by, who from all time had been the patron saint of the quarter, who had helped them through so much distress, and consoled them in so much misery? Was there not in her church that miraculous crucifix out of whose pierced side blood trickled every Good Friday, and whose hair the priests solemnly cut every Christmas,—that same crucifix which had bowed its head to avoid the enemy's bullet, and sent death to the besieger's camp and victory to Naples? And if the Madonna del Carmine could not give sufficient protection to all of them in these days of distress, had they not the venerable Madonna del Colera, who saved their city in the year 1834 from the same sickness which now raged amongst them? And in the Harbour quarter close by, did not the Madonna del Porto Salvo stand in her sumptuous chapel dressed in silk and gold brocade, ready to listen to their prayers? Was there not to be found by the Banchi Nuovi the far-famed Madonna dell'Aiuto, who would certainly not belie her name of Helper in the hour of need? Had they not La Madonna dell'Addolorata with the mantle of solid silver and the black velvet robe, whose folds no one had ever kissed without gaining comfort and peace? Had they not La Madonna dell'Immacolata, whose sky-blue garment was strewn with gold stars from the vault of heaven itself? Had they not La Madonna di Salette in her purple skirt dyed with the blood of martyrs? And did not San Gennaro himself stand in his shining dome above,—he, the patron saint of Naples, whose congealed blood flows anew every year,—he who protected the city of his care from plague and famine, and commanded the flowing lava of Vesuvius to stop before its gates? But La Madonna del Buon Cammino—who knew anything of her? Who knew whence she came or who had seen with their own eyes a single miracle worked by her hand? What kind of Madonna was that whose shrine remained without candles or flowers, and whose mantle was in rags? "*Non tiene neppure capelli, la vostra Madonna!*"[36] an old woman had once shouted in Don Dionisio's face, to the great joy of the crowd. The effect of this argument had been crushing, and Don Dionisio had disappeared in great fury inside his portico, and had not been seen again for several days.

The doctor's road lay in that direction one evening, and he determined to visit his old friend. From inside the chapel he heard Don Dionisio with mighty voice singing an old Latin hymn in honour of his Madonna.

"Consolatrix miserorum, Suscitatrix mortuorum, Mortis rumpe retia; Intendentes tuae laudi, Nos attende, nos exaudi, Nos a morte libera!"

He lifted the curtain before the door, and in the light of the little oil-lamp he saw Don Dionisio on his knees before the image of his Madonna, very busy brushing the cobwebs off an enormous old wig of an indescribable colour. His anger had not yet subsided. "*Dicono che non tiene capelli!*" he called out as soon as he caught sight of the doctor; "*mo vogliamo vedere chi tieni i più belli capelli!*"[37] And with a triumphant glance at his visitor he placed the wig upon the bald head of La Madonna del Buon Cammino. "*Come è bella, come è simpatica!*" said he, with sparkling eyes, and he arranged as well as he could the entangled curls round the forehead of the image.

When the doctor went away Don Dionisio's anger had cooled, and again he took up his position in the little portico in excellent spirits, quite ready to fight both on the offensive and defensive for his Madonna's sake. The same evening the doctor was told of a case of cholera in a *fondaco* close by the street in which Don Dionisio lived, and he went to look at it early the next morning. In passing by he saw the old fellow already at his post, rubbing his hands and looking very cheerful, and the doctor had not the heart to tell him then that even the protecting presence of his Madonna had now failed. But Don Dionisio waved his hand eagerly as soon as he caught sight of the doctor, and when he was still some distance he called out, so as to be heard throughout the whole lane, "*Ecco il colera!* See now what I have always said! Here you have got it because you would not believe in La Madonna del Buon Cammino; now you are all of you going to see what becomes of those who believe more in the Madonna del Carmine than in her! *Ecco il colera!* in our very midst, *Ecco il colera!*"

The lane was full of people, who in trembling terror had fled out of their houses to pray in the churches and before the shrines at the street corners, and some of them stopped irresolutely in front of the chapel to listen to Don Dionisio's threatening prophecy of death to every one who had dared to brave the anger of the blessed Madonna del Buon Cammino. The *fondaco* seemed quite empty, for as many as were able had run away at the first alarm; but, guided by the sound of praying voices, the doctor came at last to a dark hole, where the usual sight met his eyes. Round the door some kneeling *commare*[38] in earnest prayer; stretched out at full length upon the floor a mother wringing her hands in despair; and in a corner the livid face of a child, half-hidden under a heap of ragged coverings. The little girl was quite cold, her eyelids half shut, and her pulse scarcely perceptible. Now and again a convulsive trembling passed over her; but except for that she lay there quite motionless and insensible—cholera! At the head of the bed lay a picture of the Madonna del Carmine, and the doctor gathered from the muttering of the women that the wonder-working Madonna had been brought there the evening before. Now and then the mother lifted her head and looked searchingly at the doctor, and it seemed to him as if he could read something like confidence in her anguished eyes. And yet it appeared as if he could do nothing. Ether-injections, frictions, all the usual remedies proved fruitless to bring the warmth of life back, and the pulse grew weaker and weaker. Again the doctor saw to his surprise the same trusting expression in the mother's eyes when she looked at him, and he determined to try his new remedy. He knew well that in a case like this there was nothing to lose, for left to herself the child was evidently dying; but for some time he had been pursued by a wild idea that maybe there was everything still to gain. No one cared any longer to watch what he did; the mother lay with her forehead pressed against the floor, calling upon the Madonna with touching voice to take her own life in exchange for the child's; and amongst the *commare* the prayers had ceased and in their place a lively discussion broken out as to whether it would not be better to fetch some other Madonna, since the Madonna del Carmine would not help them in spite of all their prayers, in spite of the candles before her image, in spite of the mother's promise to dress the child in the Madonna's colour for a whole year, if only it might live. The child was quite insensible, and everything was easily done. When all was finished the doctor slightly touched the mother's shoulder, and whilst she stared at him, as if she hardly understood his words, he said that there was no time to lose if they wished to fetch another Madonna, and he suggested that they should send for the holy Madonna del Buon Cammino, whose chapel was close by. A deep silence followed his words, and it was plain that his suggestion did not meet with the smallest sympathy. He pretended to take their silence for consent, and with a little difficulty succeeded in persuading one of the women, whom he knew well, to go to the chapel of the Madonna del Buon Cammino.

Don Dionisio came like a shot with his Madonna in his arms. He put the little oil-lamp at the feet of the image, and began eagerly to sing the hymn to the honour of his Madonna, now and then casting a furious glance at the image of her powerful rival, before which the mother still lay outstretched; whilst by the door the women were muttering all sorts of opprobrious remarks about his idol: "*Vatene farti un'altra gonnella, poverella! Benedetto San Gennaro, che brutta faccia che l'hanno dato, povera vecchia!*"[39]

Suddenly they became quite silent, and in breathless amazement they all stared at the doctor's pale waxen assistant in his fight for the child's life. For from the closely compressed lips of the dying girl a subdued moan was heard, and the half-opened eyes turned slowly towards the Madonna del Buon Cammino. All crossed themselves repeatedly; and the doctor perceived the child's pulse grow stronger, and the warmth of life slowly begin to spread over the icy limbs. The terror of death began to glow in her eyes, and she cried with half-broken voice: "*Salvatemi! Salvatemi! Madonna Sanctissima!*"[40]

With a louder voice Don Dionisio began again his song of praise, and all round him now murmured the name of the blessed Madonna del Buon Cammino. Don Dionisio left the *fondaco* about an hour afterwards, followed by a procession of almost all its inhabitants. The child was then quite conscious; and all agreed that the holy Madonna del Buon Cammino had worked a miracle.

The doctor sat for a good while longer at the child's side, watching with the keenest interest the slow but sure return of its strength. Late in the evening, when he looked in again, the improvement was so marked that it was probable the child would live. Everywhere—in the *fondaco* and in the alleys around—nothing was talked of but the new miracle; and when the doctor went home he saw for the first time lights shining in the chapel of the Madonna del Buon Cammino.

He did not sleep a wink that night, for he could not keep his thoughts away from what he had witnessed in the morning, and he could hardly restrain his impatience to meet with a fresh case on which to repeat the experiment.

He had not to wait long. The same night another woman in the *fondaco* was attacked, and when he saw her the next day she was already so bad that it seemed as if she might die at any moment. His advice to fetch the Madonna del Buon Cammino was taken now without hesitation, and whilst everybody's attention was fixed upon Don Dionisio and his image, the doctor could busy himself with his patient, undisturbed by any suspicious and troublesome eyes.

Here again a speedy and decided reaction set in, which became more and more confirmed during the day; and that same evening the rumour spread through the alleys of the Mercato of a second miracle by the wonder-working Madonna del Buon Cammino.

Thus began those strange never-to-be-forgotten days, when, insensible to fatigue, yes! to hunger, the doctor went day and night from bed to bed, borne as by strong wings of an idea which almost blinded his sight, and made all his scepticism waver. He would come with Don Dionisio at his heels to meet the usual sight of some poor half-dead creature for whom it seemed as if human skill could do nothing, and when, an hour or two later, the Madonna del Buon Cammino was carried away in solemn procession, followed by the deepest devotion of the crowd, he would slip out unnoticed, forgetful of everything, in silent wonder at the sudden and constant improvement he had witnessed—an improvement which often seemed like a rising from the dead.

Ah! he had gone down there where it had seemed to him so easy to die, just as easy as it had been to delude himself with the thought that he had gone there only to help others. He had done very little for others, but a good deal for himself—he had almost forgotten his own misery. His experience of cholera was already wide enough, he knew about as much as others knew. He knew that fate reigns over death as over life. Method after method he had tried honestly and conscientiously, and he had learnt that in spite of Koch, in spite of the microbes, his ignorance was as great as ever when it came to the treatment of a cholera patient. So he had wandered round the quarters of Naples with remedies in his hands in which he did not believe himself, and words of encouragement and confidence on his lips, but hopeless scepticism in his heart.

And now this last experiment, so bold that he had almost shrunk from trying it, which had resulted in an unbroken series of successes in the midst of an epidemic with an enormous mortality! Once again he was a doctor and nothing more. With redoubled zeal he followed every case, scarcely for a minute did he leave his patient's side, and with increasing excitement he watched every symptom, every detail, with his former scepticism—and yet the fact remained, for a whole week not a single fatal case!

He had almost forgotten that Don Dionisio and the Madonna del Buon Cammino followed his footsteps—he had forgotten them as he had forgotten himself. Now and then his vacant eyes would fall upon the unconscious assistant at his side, and he felt glad that he had been able to give the old man a share in his success. Don Dionisio seemed to need no more rest than the doctor, day and night he was going about with his Madonna. His face shone with ecstasy, and he enjoyed to the full his short happiness.

The Madonna del Buon Cammino was now clothed in a flame-coloured silken mantle, a diadem of showy glass beads encircled her brow, and round her neck, strung upon a cord, hung numbers of rings and gold ear-rings. Night and day votive candles were lighted in her chapel, and on the walls, so naked before, hung *ex votos* of all possible kinds, thank-offerings for deliverance from sickness and death. The chapel was always full of people, praying fervently on their knees for help from that mighty Madonna who had performed so many miracles, and who stretched out her protecting hand over the street. For, to his amazement, the doctor had heard Don Dionisio prophesy that as long as the lights burned in the chapel of the Madonna del Buon Cammino, the cholera would never dare to approach her street.

It was now that the poor people of Naples were to suffer their deepest misery, that the infection, swift as fire, broke out all over the alleys and slums of the four poor quarters. It was now that people fell down in the street as if they had been struck by lightning; that the dying and dead lay side by side in almost every house; that the omnibuses of Portici, filled with the day's death-harvest, were driven every evening up to the Campo Santo dei Colerosi,[41] where over a thousand corpses every night filled the enormous grave. It was now that trembling hands broke down the walls with which modern times had hidden the old shrines at the street corners, that the people in wild fury stormed the Duomo to force the priests to carry San Gennaro himself down to their alleys. It was now that anxiety reached the borders of frenzy, that despair began to howl like rage, that from trembling lips prayers and curses fell in alternating confusion, that knives gleamed in hands which just before had convulsively grasped rosary and crucifix.

The doctor and his friend went on their way as before, undisturbed by the increasing terrors which surrounded them. And wherever they went Death gave way before them. The doctor needed all his self-control to enable him still to maintain his doubts, and before his eyes he saw like a mirage the goal which his daring dreams already reached. As for Don Dionisio, no questioning doubt had ever awakened his slumbering freedom of thought, and long ago the doctor had given up all attempts to restrain the old fellow's joyous conviction of his victory.

The epidemic had now reached its highest point, almost every house in the quarter was infected, and still Don Dionisio's prophecy held good, for not a single case had occurred in the street of the Madonna del Buon Cammino.

The doctor had been told by a *commare* that in one of the *bassi* in Orto del Conte lay a dying woman, and that her husband had been *avvelenato*[42] in the hospital the day before. He went there the same evening, but it was with great difficulty that he succeeded in getting through the hostile crowd which had assembled in front of the infected house. He heard that the husband had been removed almost by force to the hospital, that he had there died, and that when, a couple of hours afterwards, they had tried to remove his wife too, who had been attacked in the night, the people had opposed it, a *carabiniere* had been stabbed, and the others had had to save their lives by flight. As usual, the unfortunate doctors bore the blame of all the evil, and he heard all around him in the crowd the well-known epithets of "Ammazzacane!" "Assassino!"[43] "Avvelenatore!"[44] After several fruitless efforts to gain their confidence and make friends with them, he had no choice but to give up all attempts of helping the sick woman and to wait till Don Dionisio came. As soon as he entered the room the attention of every one was at once fixed upon him and his Madonna, and they all fell on their knees and prayed fervently, without caring in the least about either the patient or the doctor. The woman was in *Stadium algidum*,[45] but her pulse was still perceptible. Strong in the confidence of his previous successes, the doctor went to work. He had hardly finished before the heart began to flag. Just as Don Dionisio with triumphant voice announced that the miracle was done, the death-agony began, and it was with the greatest difficulty that the doctor could keep up the action of the heart until the Madonna del Buon Cammino had left the house, followed by the crowd outside in solemn procession. Shortly afterwards the doctor slipped out of the house like a thief, and ran for his life to the corner of the Via del Duomo, where he knew he would be in safety.

The same night three of his patients died. He did his utmost to prevent Don Dionisio accompanying him the following day, but in vain. Every one of the sick he visited and treated that day died under his eyes.

The wings which had borne him during those days had fallen from his shoulders, and dead tired he wandered home in the evening with Don Dionisio at his side. They said good-night to each other in front of the chapel of the Madonna del Buon Cammino, and in the flickering light of the lamp before her shrine the doctor saw a deathly pallor spread over his friend's face. The old man tottered and fell, with the Madonna in his arms. The doctor carried him into the chapel and laid him upon the straw bed where he slept, in a corner behind a curtain. He placed the Madonna del Buon Cammino carefully on her stand, and poured oil for the night into the little lamp which burned over her head. Don Dionisio motioned with his hand to be moved nearer, and the doctor dragged his bed forward to the pedestal of the image. "*Come è bella, come è simpatica!*" said he, with feeble voice. He lay there quite motionless and silent, with his eyes intently fixed upon his beloved Madonna. The doctor sat all night long by his side, whilst his strength diminished more and more and he slowly grew cold. One votive candle after another flickered and went out, and the shadows fell deeper and deeper in the chapel of the Madonna del Buon Cammino. Then it became all dark, and only the little oil-lamp as of old spread its trembling light over the pale waxen image with the impassive smile upon her rigid features.

The next day the doctor fainted in the street, and was picked up and taken to the Cholera Hospital. And, indomitable as fate, death swept over the street of the Madonna del Buon Cammino, over Vicolo del Monaco. For it was Vicolo del Monaco—that name which filled Naples with terror, and which, through the newspapers, was known to the whole world as the place where the cholera raged in its fiercest form.[46]

The dark little chapel which sheltered the old visionary's confused devotion has been razed to the ground by the new order of things which has dawned over Naples at last, and Vicolo del Monaco is no more. Don Dionisio sank unconscious from the dim thought-world of his superstition into the impenetrable darkness of the great grave up there on the Campo Santo dei Colerosi.

The other, the fool, who for a moment had believed he could command Death to stop short in his triumphant march, he is still alive, but with the bitter vision of reality for all time shadowing his sight. So will he sink, he also, into the great grave of oblivion; and of all those who lived and suffered in the Vicolo del Monaco nothing will remain—nothing.

But behind a curtain in some dark little chapel stands the Madonna del Buon Cammino, with the impassive smile upon her rigid features.

THE END

FOOTNOTES:

[1] "Toys, from the Paris Horizon" was published in *Blackwood* several years ago.

[2] This article was printed in *Murray's Magazine* several years ago.

[3] An uncanny little invention which, manipulated by hundreds of street boys, ran all along the Boulevards during the first week of the New Year. It is about the size of a thimble and costs four sous. As the Eastern question still commands the attention of Europe, we shall probably be favoured with it again this winter. To be correct, I must here state that this attractive toy is also offered for sale under the name of *Le dernier soupir de la Belle Mère*.

[4] The German toys pay, since 1871, the ridiculous duty of sixty francs per hundred kilo.

[5] The doll *à treize sous* is a characteristic Parisian type; she belongs to the family of *poupards* and is usually made of papier-mâché or wood. After the making of the head the creative power of the artist comes to a sudden stand-still; the rest of the body is only a sketch and loses itself in an oblong chaos.

[6] "This is for friends."

[7] "What nice things, what nice things, how good this milk with sugar is! Don't cry, my darling, it is ready now!"

[8] "The milk first, the milk first—never mind, take one."

[9] The lower classes in Italy still use bleeding for all kinds of diseases, and this treatment is also extended to animals. I knew a monkey in Naples who was bled twice.

[10] *Letters from a Mourning City*, by Axel Munthe. John Murray: London, 1887.

[11] "Here I stand on a rocky shore!"

[12] The old means of communication between Capri and Naples. Unfortunately replaced by an ugly little steamer.

[13] Perhaps you are not aware of the common practice in menageries of keeping a rabbit in the monkey's cage for the sake of warmth.

[14] "Is it not true that he is better to-night?"

[15] "He lies always buried in thought."

[16] "The punishment of God."

[17] "Mamma cries so."

[18] The landlord can take everything in such cases except the bed and the clothes.

[19] "Do you know, doctor?"

[20] Scoundrels and poisoners.

[21] The then manager of the Théâtre Français.

[22] "*Il met son bonnet*"—the guides' usual and sufficiently characteristic metaphor referring to that little cloud which suddenly covers the summit of Mont Blanc—it announces a storm. It looks its best from a certain distance.

[23] Heine.

[24] The harbour of refuge for most of the shipwrecked ones who still can and will work. The street scavengers of Paris are to a great extent Italians.

[25] I was for ten years the confidant, the friend, and the doctor to most of the poor Italians in Paris, the greater number of whom are models. My experience during these years was a terrible one. Nine years in Rome have made the evidence still more conclusive. Of English models I know nothing and have nothing to say.

[26] I write here as I talk here—not Italian but Capri dialect. The old Emperor, who lived on the island for eleven years, is never called Tiberio here, but "Timberio."

[27] Our friend old Mr. X——, for fifteen years the delight and ornament of the Piazza of Capri, always cheerful, always thirsty, a great destroyer of quails and wine-bottles, now at last gone to rest in the quiet little field outside the town of Capri, where the sombre green of some laurel and cypress-trees stands out between the waving branches of his favourite plant, the vine. Old Spadaro is still alive, and will tell you all about his lamented master.

[28] Quail bishop. Capri no longer owns a bishop, but the quail harvest still forms one—and perhaps the most important—item of the island's revenue.

[29] Few strangers visit the grotto of Mitromania, the name of which may be derived from *Magnum Mitrae Antrum*. It faces east, and the first rays of the sun light up its mysterious gloom. One knows from excavations made here that once upon a time the old, yet ever young, sun-god was worshipped in this cave.

[30] Leopardi.

[31] Pumaroli-pomidoro, *i.e.* tomato, the Southern Italian's favourite fruit, the most important ingredient in everything he eats, sweetening the monotony of his macaroni.

[32] "Let us be off."

[33] The alarm-bell used to be rung from the old tower to warn the shores of the gulf of the approach of pirates.

[34] "How beautiful, how sympathetic she is!"

[35] "Madonna del Carmine indeed!"

[36] "Your Madonna has not even got any hair on her head!"

[37] "They say she has got no hair! but we shall soon see who has the most beautiful hair!"

[38] Gossips.

[39] "Go and make thyself another gown, poor thing! Blessed San Gennaro, what an ugly face they have given her, poor old creature!"

[40] "Save me, save me, most holy Madonna!"

[41] Cholera cemetery.

[42] Poisoned.

[43] "Dog-murderer!" "Assassin!"

[44] "Poisoner!"

[45] The state of collapse, characteristic of cholera, when the body becomes cold.

[46] Almost the whole alley died. An official report stated that there were over thirty cases in a single hour.

Milton Keynes UK
Ingram Content Group UK Ltd.
UKHW030742071024
449371UK00006B/627

9 789362 092830